NECESSARY NOISES
AN INTRODUCTION TO ENGLISH PHONOLOGY

STEVE BUCKLEDEE

Published 2007 by abramis

www.abramis.com

ISBN 978-1-84549-249-6

© Steve Buckledee 2007

All rights reserved

This book is copyright. Subject to statutory exception and to provisions of relevant collective licensing agreements, no part of this publication may be reproduced, stored in a retrieval system, or transmitted in any form or by any means, without the prior written permission of the author.

Printed and bound in the United Kingdom & USA

This book is sold subject to the conditions that it shall not, by way of trade or otherwise, be lent, re-sold, hired out, or otherwise circulated without the publisher's prior consent in any form of binding or cover other than that which it is published and without a similar condition including this condition being imposed on the subsequent purchaser.

abramis is an imprint of arima publishing

arima publishing
ASK House, Northgate Avenue
Bury St Edmunds, Suffolk IP32 6BB, UK
t: (+44) 01284 700321

www.arimapublishing.com

CONTENTS

Preface	4
1 Jargon-Busting: essential terminology explained	7
2 Pops and Fizzes: the consonants of English	11
3 Shaping Air: vowels and diphthongs	19
4 Bruisers and Wimps: syllables, stress and rhythm	25
5 Joined-Up Talk: features of connected speech	33
6 Attitudes and Feelings: the functions of intonation	39
7 Right Watt Ewe Here: pronunciation and spelling	47
8 Disgusted of Tunbridge Wells: how English pronunciation is changing	53
Key to Tasks	61
Suggestions for Further Reading	71
Index	73

PREFACE

This book is, as the title explicitly states, an introduction. It deals with the essential features of English phonology for people who have little or no previous knowledge of the subject, and it endeavours to present those key aspects in a way that the reader will find clear and engaging. The target readers could be native speakers of English seeking an accessible introduction to the field, perhaps with a view to teaching English, or students of English as a foreign language who require something a little more technical than the pronunciation practice conducted in the EFL classroom.

We are all guilty of making value judgements about what different languages, or different varieties of the same language, sound like: Italian is musical, Danish sounds like someone gargling, Irish English is lilting, Midlands English is ugly and so on. The first lesson the student of phonology must learn is to eliminate, or at least suppress, such subjective and scientifically unsustainable views. Among the many regional and social varieties of English, no accent is "better" than any other; if the pronunciation of Boston, Massachusetts enjoys far greater prestige in the United States than that of Montgomery, Alabama, the reasons have everything to do with history, politics and economics and nothing at all to do with the intrinsic qualities of the two sound systems. That said, the non-native speaker expects to be given the variety of the target language that has the highest social status, and for that reason the pronunciation model adopted in this work is RP, the prestige accent of the United Kingdom. RP stands for Received Pronunciation (although many commentators have noted that it could just as easily mean Really Posh), and is the regionally neutral accent associated with higher education and BBC newsreaders. This does not imply, however, that students of English as a foreign language should be sheltered from other pronunciation models (after all, only a small minority of British people speak this prestige variety), nor that native-speaker teachers of English should try to replace their regional accents with RP. In the final analysis all accents, whatever their "respectability" in society, are just sets of noises. Necessary noises, however, for without them we would never have developed as a species.

S.B.
Cagliari, 2007.

ACKNOWLEDGEMENT

In Chapter 7 of this work the first eight lines of Gerald Nolst Trenité's poem *The Chaos* have been quoted. The author has been unable to contact the current copyright owner of this work and would be pleased to receive any information that would enable him to do so.

Chapter 1
JARGON-BUSTING

Why pronunciation is important

> On a visit to the USA, President Charles de Gaulle of France and his wife were invited to a banquet at the White House. To make small-talk, an official asked his wife, "Madame de Gaulle, what do you think the most important thing in life is?"
> "A penis," she replied.
> Overhearing, her husband informed her, "I think, my dear, that in English it is pronounced 'appiness."
> (Probably an urban legend, but a nice one.)

Think about it

> If English is your second language, think about what your targets are as regards your own pronunciation of English. Are you happy with the pronunciation you have now or do you hope to improve it? Do you think it is necessary to start learning a language at an early age to develop good pronunciation? Then read the *Key to Tasks* section at the back of this book.
>
> If you are a teacher of English, what do you consider "acceptable" pronunciation for your students? Do you find that some students are reluctant to do work on pronunciation practice in the classroom? Then turn to the *Key to Tasks* section.

Essential Terminology

Phonology or Phonetics?

It is important to distinguish between these two terms. Phonetics is the study of speech sounds – their articulatory, acoustic and auditory characteristics – without direct reference to how those sounds are used in language. Phonology also studies speech sounds but in relation to their linguistic functions and communicative purposes. In this work there are descriptions of how sounds are produced that belong to the field of phonetics, but most of the book is concerned with how sounds

– or necessary noises – operate in the context of the English language, so this text is primarily concerned with phonology.

Phonemes and Allophones

Phonemes are the smallest units of sound within a language that can effect a change in meaning (the term is analogous to *morpheme*, the minimal unit of a grammatical system). For example, the English sounds represented by the letters *t* and *d* are phonemes because although there are similarities in how they are articulated, substituting one for the other will change meaning (compare *town* with *down*). Allophones are perceptible differences in the realisation of a phoneme which do not affect meaning. Many people in the south of England use a breathy, aspirated *p* in a word like *pal* but in Yorkshire the same word is pronounced without aspiration. The two types of *p* – represented by the symbols /pʰ/ and /p/ – are allophones that tell us something about the speaker's background but which do not influence our comprehension of the word uttered. As we will see later, a pair of sounds may be separate phonemes in one language but mere allophones in another.

IPA vs Phonemic Transcription

Phoneticians use the International Phonetic Alphabet (IPA) to transcribe the huge number of sounds that human beings produce in their languages. A work of this nature does not require such a precise and detailed system of transcription. Phonemic transcription, which represents phonemes but does not indicate allophonic variations, will be employed. For example, the phonemic transcription of the word *rat* is /ræt/ even though most English speakers (with the obvious exception of the Scots) do not use the rolled or trill *r* that /r/ truly indicates.

The Articulators of Speech

All the phonemes of English start with exhalation. Some languages, Swahili for example, also have sounds that involve inhalation but exhalation is the norm because, as all swimmers know, it is much easier to control the air that we breathe out than that which we breathe in. As air passes through the vocal tract, various organs of speech, or *articulators*, come into play. The air may be directed in some way, or blocked, or partially blocked.

Starting with the most external articulators, the *lips* and *teeth* are fundamental. Nowadays one rarely encounters a person who has lost all their teeth and does not use dentures, but one of the long-term consequences of neglecting to brush one's teeth is the distortion of certain speech sounds. The *nose* is required for some phonemes, and when you have a blocked nose caused by a cold, those sounds are not articulated properly. Run your tongue behind your upper front teeth and you will feel your *alveolar ridge*, and behind that what is commonly called the roof of the mouth, or *hard palate*. Curling your tongue back as much as you can, you can just feel your *soft palate*, or *velum*. Finally, there are the articulators that you can neither see nor touch: the *vocal cords* and the opening between them, which is called the *glottis*. Phonetic descriptions of how sounds are produced require the use of the adjectives related to the various articulators: *labial* (related to lip) or *bilabial* if both lips are involved, *dental*, *nasal*, *alveolar*, *palatal*, *velar* and *glottal*.

Vital factors in the production of our necessary noises are the position of the tongue in relation to other articulators and the part of the tongue that is involved. There is no problem in referring to the *tip* and the *back* of the tongue. Between the tip and the back, we have the *blade* – the part we use to lick an icecream – and the *front*. This use of "front" seems somewhat illogical at first when we consider that both the tip and the blade are actually "in front of the front" (the order is tip – blade – front – back).

These are the articulators required to produce the phonemes of RP. Some languages, and indeed some varieties of English, involve other articulators (the characteristic French *r*, for instance, is produced when the back of the tongue approaches the *uvula*, the grape-like organ dangling at the back of the mouth) but one of the aims of this book is not to overload the reader with terminology that is not strictly necessary.

Chapter 2
POPS AND FIZZES

Think about it

"Brute animals have the vowel sounds; man only can utter consonants."
Samuel Taylor Coleridge

Try this...

> but in the privacy of your own home rather than in public.
>
> Place a finger in each ear and make a sssssss noise like the hissing of a snake. Then make a zzzzzzz noise like the buzzing of a fly. What do you notice?

When imitating a fly you will have heard a noise in your head that was not present when you were being a snake. That is the phenomenon of *voicing*, which is caused by vibration of the vocal cords. The snake's hiss (phonemic symbol /s/) involves no vibration of the vocal cords and is known as an *unvoiced*, a *voiceless* or a *fortis* consonant. In this work the term *unvoiced* will be used. The buzzing of the fly (/z/) requires vibration and is a *voiced* or a *lenis* consonant.

You can place your fingers in your ears and try the same experiment with ffffffff and vvvvvvvv, and you will see that the same unvoiced/voiced distinction holds true for /f/ and /v/. Once again, the phonemic symbols correspond with letters of the Roman alphabet, but that is not always the case. The letters *th* represent an unvoiced consonant (/θ/) in words such as *thick* and *thin*, but a voiced consonant (/ð/) in *this* and *that*. Another unvoiced/voiced pair is /ʃ/ as in *ship* and /ʒ/, which in English never occurs in initial position in a word but is found in medial position in *measure* and *leisure*.

One definition of the word *consonant* is that it is a sound that involves some kind of obstruction or hindrance to the air that passes through the vocal tract. The consonants considered so far have an important feature in common: in each case the articulators create a partial obstruction, which produces friction, so they are called *fricatives*. We now have to consider how that partial obstruction is established in each case.

Repeat the ffffffff and vvvvvvvv experiment and note what you are doing with your lips and your teeth. For both /f/ and /v/ your lower lip is in contact with your upper teeth and the air has to force its way out through the partial closure. If it is a lip/teeth contact, we can describe these two consonants as *labiodental fricatives*, one unvoiced and the other voiced.

Prolonging the /θ/ and /ð/ sounds makes us aware that now the contact is between the tip of the tongue and the upper teeth, so these are *dental* or some prefer *linguo-dental fricatives*. Some learners have difficulties with these consonants and tend to say *fink* instead of *think* (as indeed do many Londoners when they use their Cockney accent) but it is actually quite easy for a teacher to demonstrate the remedy because the points of articulation of both /f/ and /θ/ are clearly visible. Interestingly, Cockneys who do not pronounce unvoiced /θ/ tend to say its voiced partner /ð/ correctly when it is in initial position (in *that* or *those*) but use another voiced consonant, /v/, in medial position (*mother* becomes *muvver*).

For /s/ and /z/ the point of contact is a little further back on the alveolar ridge, so it will come as no surprise to learn that they are classed as *alveolar fricatives*. Then for /ʃ/ and /ʒ/ the contact is still further back as the front of the tongue (which, you will remember, is actually behind the tip and the blade) is raised towards an area between the alveolar ridge and the hard palate. To become aware of the position of the tongue, try alternating alveolar /s/ and the *palato-alveolar fricative* /ʃ/ several times. Slightly less effort and control is required to articulate with the front of the tongue than with the tip, which might well explain why drunks sometimes use /ʃ/ and /ʒ/ instead of /s/ and /z/.

The last of the RP fricatives is the aspirated *h* represented by the symbol /h/. If you produce an extended hhhhhhhh you will notice that the tongue, lips and teeth do absolutely nothing to obstruct the flow of air as it passes through the vocal tract, so this sound scarcely qualifies as a consonant at all. Yet partial obstruction takes place, but it occurs in a place that we cannot see or feel. We define /h/ as a *glottal fricative* because the obstruction occurs in the glottis, the space between the vocal cords. The vocal cords do not close completely (no sound would emerge at all if they did) but there is sufficient narrowing to create friction and thus produce the breathy sound of this consonant.

Think about it

To help you understand what happens with the articulation of fricatives, you were asked to practise extended sounds: ffffffff, zzzzzzzz, hhhhhhhh etc. Now think of some consonant sounds that are impossible to extend.

POPS AND FIZZES

Another category of consonants is that of the *plosives*, and once again we have unvoiced and voiced pairs. While fricatives are *continuants* – fizzes, buzzes and hisses that can be extended – plosives are pops, taps and knocks that are over in a fraction of a second. They are, as their name suggests, little explosions, and they are produced by a total rather than partial obstruction of air followed by a sudden release. There are three unvoiced/voiced pairs of plosives in RP, and all six consonants are represented by phonemic symbols that correspond to the letters of the alphabet associated with these sounds.

Unvoiced /p/ and voiced /b/ both involve the build-up of pressure behind the lips then the release of the trapped air. They are *bilabial plosives*. As mentioned in the previous chapter, when /p/ is in initial position, it is aspirated to /p^h/ by many English speakers. Because the lips have to close to produce these sounds, it is no coincidence that they are the consonants that create most difficulty for would-be ventriloquists.

The /t/ and /d/ pair are *alveolar plosives*. Unlike the alveolar fricatives /s/ and /z/ which involve a partial obstruction that allows air to force its way through a narrow opening, for /t/ and /d/ the blade of the tongue presses firmly against the alveolar ridge to create a complete obstruction. As with /p/, initial /t/ is aspirated to /t^h/ in some varieties of English.

You will need to practise /k/ and /g/ a few times to feel what is happening. The back of the tongue is raised and forms an obstruction by pressing against the soft palate or velum, so they are *velar plosives*.

There are two RP consonants that bridge the gap between plosives and fricatives. They are the two *affricates*, unvoiced /tʃ/, the initial sound in *chalk* and *cheese*, and voiced /dʒ/, as in *judge* and *jury*. If you say *what shop* as quickly as you can, you will note that the final /t/ of *what* merges with the initial /ʃ/ of *shop* so that the *shop* sounds like a *chop*. The point of articulation of /tʃ/ and /dʒ/ is slightly behind that of alveolar /t/ and /d/, so they are classed as *palato-alveolar* consonants.

RP has three *nasal consonants*: /m/, /n/ and /ŋ/. The first of these is easy to describe: air has to be expelled through the nose because the lips are tightly shut, so it is a *bilabial consonant*. For /n/ you can feel that the blade of your tongue touches the alveolar ridge (hence it is an *alveolar consonant*), but unlike the case of the alveolar plosives /t/ and /d/, the obstruction is maintained so that air is forced to escape via the nose rather than the mouth. The most difficult one to describe is /ŋ/, a consonant that appears in medial or final positions but never at the beginning of a word in English, and which is represented by the alphabetical letters *ng* in such terms as *wrong*, *hung* or *singer*. Like /k/ and /g/, /ŋ/ is a *velar consonant* because the back of the tongue is raised towards the velum, or soft palate. There is no sudden release, which would produce a plosive, so once again air has to exit from the nose.

In non-RP realisations /n/ sometimes replaces /ŋ/ in final position. The convention in writing is to use an apostrophe to indicate an omitted *g*, as in the Cockney barrow boy's *wheelin' and dealin'* (though the phenomenon also occurs in the speech of quite different social classes, as evinced in the aristocratic affectation of *huntin', shootin' and fishin'*). In reality the use of an apostrophe for omission is wrong since there was never a /g/ (as opposed to the letter *g*) there in the first place; quite simply, one nasal consonant has taken the place of another. The pronunciation of *ng* is problematical, however, since sometimes we say /ŋg/, as in *finger*, and sometimes it is just /ŋ/, as in *winger* (not to mention the /dʒ/ of *whinger*). There is, in fact, a rule to explain the issue of /ŋg/ or /ŋ/ in medial position: while *winger* consists of two morphemes – *wing* + *er* – *finger* is a single morpheme, and /ŋ/ rather than /ŋg/ is used at the end of a morpheme. Similarly, the two-morpheme *banger* is pronounced with /ŋ/ while the one-morpheme *anger* has /ŋg/.

Think about it

Just look what the unruly daughters of Mother Latin have been up to:		
Spanish	*Portuguese*	*Italian*
Blanco	branco	bianco
Plaza	praça	piazza
Plato	prato	piatto
And on the same subject, what is the difference between the English words *crash* and *clash*? How are they translated into other languages?		

Two consonants that should be considered together are /l/ and /r/. They create difficulties for many learners of English, and before we make fun of our Japanesese students who eat lice and have erections every five years, we might reflect upon the problems Europeans have had with them over the centuries.

The consonant represented by the letter *r* has a number of realisations. The strong rolled or trill *r* of Italian or Scots English is described as a *retroflex consonant* because its articulation requires that the tongue be curled backwards with the tip raised. The trill effect is produced by a rapid and repeated tapping of the tip of the tongue against the hard palate. It is by no means an easy sound to produce, and people whose native language does not have retroflex *r* often find that they never manage to acquire it as they endeavour to learn a second language in which it occurs. Indeed, even some native speakers fail to master this consonant; several prominent Italians have enjoyed great success in their various fields but have failed miserably to curl back their tongue and rattle it against their palate.

As mentioned earlier, the characteristic *grasséyé r* of French is an *uvular consonant*. This too is a difficult sound for non-French speakers to acquire. Furthermore, once acquired, it is difficult to modify; French people who otherwise have excellent command of a second language are often betrayed by their *r*.

The RP version is a weak, pathetic creature in comparison with the lusty rolled *r*. Indeed, phoneticians describe it as an *approximant* since it does not fully meet the essential requirement to be classified as a consonant, i.e. some kind of obstruction in the flow of air from the larynx to the lips. Even its phonetic symbol, /ɹ/, suggests that it isn't much of an *r* at all. As with /r/ (rolled *r*), RP *r* involves curling back the tongue and raising the tip towards the palate. The essential difference, however, is that no actual contact is made between tongue and palate, so complete obstruction does not occur. The tongue gets very close to the position required to realise /r/ but does not quite complete the journey, and it is this incompletion that labels RP *r* as an approximant. The resulting sound has some of the indefinite quality of a vowel; indeed, by rounding the lips a little the English *r* can be made to sound very close to the semivowel (see below) /w/. As mentioned earlier, in this work RP *r* is transcribed using the phonemic symbol /r/ even though it does not truly represent the way most English speakers articulate the consonant.

The distribution of *r* is one of the essential factors distinguishing RP from American English (and, indeed, from the English spoken in Ireland and in the south-west of England itself). In RP *r* is only pronounced in pre-vowel position while in American and other varieties of English it may be retained before a pause or before a consonant in words like *car* and *cart*. The modal verb *may* is used advisedly, however, for some US citizens do not pronounce post-vocalic *r*. In the 1960s the sociolinguist William Labov conducted experiments in New York department stores in which shoppers were asked questions to which the answer was always "fourth floor". He found that the incidence of post-vocalic *r* was related to social class: the posher the store, and therefore the higher the social class of the shoppers, the greater the incidence of pronounced *r* in *fourth* and *floor*. In the 1970s the British sociolinguist Peter Trudgill replicated Labov's study in the English city of Norwich. Trudgill also found a link with social class, but in his experiments the relationship was reversed: the higher the social class, the greater the likelihood that *r* would not be pronounced.

Moving on to /l/, this is classified as a *lateral consonant* because its articulation involves contact between the tongue and the alveolar ridge which causes a closure that forces exhaled air to escape along the two sides rather than the centre of the tongue. In many languages /l/ is always articulated in that way regardless of its distribution (i.e. its pre- or post-vowel/consonant position). A feature of RP is that the phoneme /l/ has two allophones, known as *clear l* and *dark l* respectively. Clear *l* is articulated as described above and in RP it occurs when /l/ precedes a vowel. With dark *l* the back of the tongue is raised towards the soft palate, thus giving the consonant a velarised quality that contrasts with the palatised sound of clear *l*. In RP dark *l* typically occurs after a vowel and before a consonant or a pause. Native speakers of English can become aware of the variation in tongue position by repeating the words *look*, which has clear *l*, and *cool*, which has dark *l*. Pre-vowel clear *l* is used in *love* and *glove*, while dark *l* is used before a consonant in *milk* and before a pause in *call*. *Bull* has dark *l* but the addition of a vowel in *bullet* requires the use of clear *l*.

Non-native speakers may find it difficult to perceive the difference between clear and dark *l*, never mind make the distinction in their own production. Those intent on trying should start from considering the way the back of the tongue is raised towards the soft palate in velar /ŋ/. In practice, many learners of English use clear *l* in all positions, and since inappropriate allophones do not prejudice meaning, no one bothers to correct them. However, the absence of dark *l* will give their speech a foreign quality that all native speakers can detect though few can explain. In the same way we can detect a difference between the way French people say *mille* and the British say *meal*. The English word has a slightly longer vowel, but an equally significant difference is that the French use clear *l* and the English dark *l*.

So why do *l* and *r* create so much confusion? To begin with, their points of articulation are very close, alveolar for /l/ and palato-alveolar for /r/. It is, however, quite easy to pronounce a recognisable /l/ with the tongue touching the palate rather than the alveolar ridge, and awkward but possible to produce rolled /r/ with tapping of the tongue further forward against the alveolar ridge. With /l/ the tongue caresses the alveolar ridge but /r/ necessitates fast and repeated tapping. In a sense, therefore, what really distinguishes these two sounds is not so much the position of articulation but the degree of force applied, so a tired or lazy realisation of /r/ could sound close to /l/, while an overenthusiastic /l/ might be perceived as /r/. Confusion between the two seldom occurs when they are in initial position, but as we have seen with those wayward daughters of Mother Latin, when they follow another consonant, odd things can happen. I am reminded of this phenomenon on a daily basis since I live in a place in Sardinia that one roadsign indicates as Flumini Cuba while another, some 100 metres further on and erected by the same public body, calls Frumini Cuba. I can also recall a period during my childhood when I was convinced that God's first name was Harold. The misunderstanding stemmed from hearing people say the Lord's prayer in church: 'Our father, who art in heaven, Harold be thy name…'

The last two consonants are /w/ and /j/. The latter must not be confused with the alphabetical letter *j*, which in English is usually pronounced as /dʒ/; /j/ represents the initial sound in *yellow* and *York*. Like RP *r*, these two phonemes are classed as *approximants* (or some phoneticians prefer to describe them as *semivowels*) because they involve hardly any obstruction to the air passing through the vocal tract. From a purely phonetic point of view they are not really consonants at all, but they tend to be classified as consonants for phonological reasons, i.e. because of how they function within the context of the English language. They behave like consonants in significant ways. Firstly, nouns beginning with /w/ or /j/ are preceded by the indefinite article *a*, not *an*. A second feature typical of consonants is that they only occur before vowel phonemes (the alphabetical letter *w* can precede a consonant in *write* or precede a pause in *how*, but in neither case is it pronounced as /w/). We must purse the lips to produce /w/, so it is *bilabial*, while for /j/ we raise the tongue towards the hard palate without actually making contact, which makes it closer to a *palatal* consonant than anything else.

Over to you

Try to complete this chart. If there is an unvoiced/voiced pair, place the unvoiced phoneme to the left. Do not include allophones. When you have finished, turn to the *Key to Tasks* section at the back of this book.

The Consonant Phonemes of Received Pronunciation

	Bilabial	Labiodental	Linguo-dental	Alveolar	Palato-alveolar	Palatal	Velar	Glottal
Fricative		f v						
Plosive								
Affricate								
Nasal								
Lateral								
Approximant								

Chapter 3
SHAPING AIR

Think about it

We are little airy creatures,
All of different voice and features;
One of us in glass is set,
One of us you'll find in jet,
T'other you may see in tin,
And the fourth a box within.
If the fifth you should pursue,
It can never fly from you.
Jonathan Swift

Long and short vowels

What characterises our next necessary noises, the vowels, is that there is no obstruction to the air that flows through the vocal tract. It is never trapped or made to force its way through a narrow opening, although it is directed and, in a certain sense, shaped by the tongue and lips.

If voicing is an important criterion in the description of consonants, for vowels a fundamental consideration is that of length. Let's begin with a pair of vowels that represent a potential minefield for people using English as a second language: the short /ɪ/ of *bit*, *pill* and *whip* and the long /iː/ of *beat*, *peel* and *weep*.

In Chapter One we noted that distinct sounds that are phonemes in one language may be mere allophones in another. From the examples given above, it is obvious that /ɪ/ and /iː/ are phonemes in English because swapping one for the other triggers a radical change in meaning. In many languages, however, there is just one *i* vowel, which may vary in length according to regional or social dialect but such variations are allophonic and do not influence meaning. If I pronounce the word *pizza* with a short /ɪ/ in a restaurant in Rome, the waiter might smile at my mispronunciation but will nevertheless understand what I want. In English, on the other hand, incorrect vowel length could lead to surreal references to personal trainers who help us kip feet, entrepreneurs who make takeover beads and politicians who promise us piss and prosperity.

It is an oversimplification to talk of just two realisations of the *i* vowel. The vowel in *beat* is clearly longer than that in *bit*, but the one in *bead* is longer still. Similarly, there is a short vowel in *lick*, a long one in *leak* and an even longer one in

NECESSARY NOISES

league. The reason is that /iː/ is longer when it precedes voiced consonants like /d/ and /g/ than it is before their unvoiced partners /t/ and /k/. A phonetic transcription would make this distinction apparent but a phonemic transcription does not.

Now let's look at some more short vowels and long vowels.

Ham, *cat* and *pack* have the short vowel /æ/. We can transcribe the complete words as /hæm/, /kæt/ and /pæk/.

Harm, *car* and *park* have the long vowel /ɑː/. The transcriptions are /hɑːm/, /kɑː/ and /pɑːk/.

Cot, *hod* and *sot* have the short /ɒ/.   /kɒt/   /hɒd/   /sɒt/
Caught, *horde* and *sort* have the long /ɔː/.   /kɔːt/   /hɔːd/   /sɔːt/

Over to you 1

> By now you will have noted that in phonemic transcription long vowels are indicated by ː but there is also an indicator in the writing system. Try to discover what it is. Then go to to the *Key to Tasks* section.

Book, *foot* and *put* have the short vowel /ʊ/.   /bʊk/   /fʊt/   /pʊt/
Boot, *cute* and *rude* have the long vowel /uː/.   /buːt/   /kjuːt/   /ruːd/

By far the most frequently uttered vowel in English is /ə/, which is known as *schwa* or *shwa*. It is an indistinct sound that is represented in the writing system by various letters and combinations of letters. It can appear in initial, medial or final position. The underlined syllables in the following words all feature schwa: *the*, *about*, *water*, *circus*, *fracture*, *category*, *intermediate*. As we will see in the next chapter, /ə/ is typically used in unstressed syllables.

The long partner of schwa is /ɜː/, which in the writing system is often indicated by *o + r* (*word*), *i + r* (*shirt*), *u + r* (*hurt*), *e + r* (*term*) or *ea + r* (*heard*). Some dictionaries indicate both the RP and the American pronunciations of these words, so *third* will be transcribed as /θɜːd/ for the former and /θɜːʳd/ or /θɜːrd/ for the latter.

There are two more short vowels: /e/ as in *bed*, *said* or past tense *read*, and /ʌ/ which is often represented by the letter *u* (*but*, *mud* etc.) or by *oo* (*blood*, *flood* etc.). It can also be the vowel in that baffling combination of letters *ough* (*tough* = /tʌf/, *rough* = /rʌf/).

Other ways to describe vowels

Length is not the only thing to consider when we describe vowels and how they are produced. The role of the lips is important: a vowel such as /uː/ is made with the lips rounded, for /iː/ the lips must be spread , while /ə/ can be made with the lips in a neutral position, i.e. neither rounded nor spread.

The position of the tongue is another factor to take into account. The tip and the blade of the tongue are vital for the articulation of certain consonants, but for vowels we are interested in the front and the back.

Try this

> Stand in front of a mirror and study the position of your tongue as you say /iː/ then /e/ then /æ/. Do it several times.

You will have seen that when producing /iː/ your tongue was practically hidden behind your upper teeth. Some phoneticians describe /iː/ as a *close* vowel because the front of the tongue is close to the hard palate. Others prefer to call it a *high* vowel because the front of the tongue is in a high position. We will use *close* in this work.

As you observed yourself saying /e/ you should have noticed that the distance between your tongue and your palate increased, then it increased further and your jaw dropped when you said /æ/. So /æ/ is an *open* (or a *low*) vowel. Between the close and open poles we have *half-close* and *half-open* vowels.

It was easy to observe your tongue movements while practising /iː/ + /e/ + /æ/ because they are produced with the lips spread and they involve the front of the tongue. We cannot see what is happening when we say /uː/ + /ɔː/ + /ɑː/ because the lips are rounded for the first two and all three involve the back of the tongue. With practice, however, it is possible to feel that the back of the tongue is close to the velum for /uː/, that /ɔː/ is half-close and that /ɑː/ is an open vowel. Vowels can be described, therefore, in terms of *front* and *back* (the part of the tongue) as well as in terms of *close* and *open* (the height of the tongue).

With a vowel like /iː/ we can actually see that it is close and front. With /ɑː/ it is not difficult to feel that it is open and back. Others are neither front nor back but *central*, while some are difficult to locate on the close/open scale. The most indefinite vowels of all are /ʌ/, /ɜː/ and /ə/. The following chart describe RP vowels according to tongue height, lip formation and whether they are front or back.

Fig. 3.1

	Front/Back	Close/Open	Lips
/iː/	Front	Close	Slightly spread
/ɪ/	Front, slightly less so than /iː/	Close, slightly less so than /iː/	Slightly spread
/e/	Front	Midway between close and open	Slightly spread
/æ/	Front	Open	Slightly spread
/ɒ/	Back	Between half-open and open	Slightly rounded
/ɔː/	Back	Midway between close and open	Rounded
/uː/	Back	Close	Fairly rounded
/ʊ/	Back, less so than /uː/	Between close and half-close	Rounded
/ʌ/	Central	Between open and half-open	Neutral
/ɜː/	Central	Between close and open	Neutral
/ə/	Central	Between close and open	Neutral

Diphthongs

Our necessary noises are a sociable lot and seem to enjoy getting together. Consonants often pair up (*plan* /plæn/), form groups of three (*strip* /strɪp/) or even four (*strengths* /streŋkθs/). These groupings are called *consonant clusters*. When two vowels get together they form a *diphthong*. In effect, one vowel moves, or *glides*, towards another.

Three diphthongs glide towards /ɪ/: /e/ glides towards /ɪ/ to form /eɪ/, which we hear in *day* and *hate*; /æ/ and /ɪ/ form /aɪ/, as in *my* and *light*; and /ɔ/ travels towards /ɪ/ to make the /ɔɪ/ that we hear in *toy* and *boy*.

Three others glide towards schwa to give us /ɪə/ (*ear, here*), /eə/ (*air, care*) and /ʊə/ (*pure, tour*).

Finally, two diphthongs head for /ʊ/: /aʊ/, as in *now* and *out*, and /əʊ/ as in *know* and *so*.

Sometimes schwa is added to a diphthong to form a *triphthong*. Examples can be heard in words such as *player* (/pleɪə/), *fire* (/faɪə/), *royal* (/rɔɪəl/), *hour* (/aʊə/) and *lower* (/ləʊə/).

SHAPING AIR

The following table shows all the vowels and diphthongs of RP.

Fig. 3.2

Short vowels	Long vowels	Diphthongs
ɪ	iː	eɪ
æ	ɑː	aɪ
ɒ	ɔː	ɔɪ
ə	ɜː	ɪə
ʊ	uː	ʊə
e		eə
ʌ		aʊ
		əʊ

Over to you 2

Write the words indicated by these transcriptions. Then go to *Key to Tasks* to check.

1 /tʃɜːtʃ/ _____

2 /fɒks/ _____

3 /luːz/ _____

4 /helθ/ _____

5 /jeləʊ/ _____

6 /rɪŋ/ _____

7 /kʌt/ _____

8 /ðəʊz/ _____

9 /kraɪ/ _____

10 /dʒɔː/ _____

NECESSARY NOISES

Over to you 3

Now the difficult part. Try to write the phonemic transcriptions of these words, then check the *Key to Tasks* section.

A note on transcription: when the letter *y* is in final position and therefore functions as a vowel, it is longer than /ɪ/ but shorter than /iː/, so the convention is to use /i/ without the ː diacritic. For example, the phonemic transcription of *easy* is /iːzi/.

1 near _____
2 size _____
3 butter _____
4 look _____
5 thirty _____

6 need _____
7 hair _____
8 rather _____
9 early _____
10 wash _____

Chapter 4
BRUISERS AND WIMPS

Think about it 1

"Syllables govern the world."
George Bernard Shaw

Think about it 2

Look at these sentences and consider the pronunciation of the words printed in italics. Then go to the *Key to Exercises* section.

1a. What a lovely *present*! Thankyou.
1b. It is my honour to *present* you with this token of our gratitude.
2a. Her exam was *perfect*. She got an A+ grade.
2b. He's going to Lisbon to *perfect* his spoken Portuguese.
3a. He's the *rebel* of the school. He's always questioning the system.
3b. They tried to *rebel* but the invading army was too strong

So we can divide syllables into bruisers and wimps, the strong and the weak, the stressed and the unstressed. Our first problem is to decide how many syllables there are in a word. With languages that have a phonetic spelling system, such as Spanish and Italian, you can just look at the written word and count the syllables, but in the English orthographic system there is often no direct relationship between spelling and pronunciation. We have to rely on our perceptions of how a word is said, but perceptions are subjective, and in any case native speakers do not all produce the word in the same way. Ask a small group of native speakers of English to count and identify the syllables in *Wednesday* and a heated debate is likely to develop. Is it /ˈwenzdeɪ/, a two-syllable word with the first *d* silent? Or is it /ˈwed(ə)nzdeɪ/, a three-syllable word with the first *d* pronounced? Dictionaries tend to indicate the first as the preferred option but some offer the second as a legitimate alternative. Some also suggest a third possibility: /ˈwenzdɪ/.
    What is a syllable? It is essentially a unit of *rhythm*, and is the minimal unit in the organisation of sounds in sequence. The *minimal syllable* has no more than an obligatory *nucleus*, which in English is generally a vowel in isolation; the article *a* and the verb *are*, for instance, are minimal syllables, /ə/ and /ɑː/ respectively.

That part of a syllable that precedes the nucleus, typically a consonant, is called the *onset*. *Far* is composed of a syllable consisting of onset + nucleus: /fɑː/. A syllable ending in a vowel is known as an *open syllable*.

Sometimes syllables do not have an onset but have a *termination* instead, i.e. something, again usually a consonant, after the nucleus, as in *at* (/æt/) or *if* (/ɪf/). A syllable ending in a consonant is a *closed syllable*.

Syllables frequently have both an onset and a termination, as in *pig* (/pɪg/). In the last chapter we looked briefly at consonant clusters and one of the examples given was the monosyllabic word *strengths*. That word demonstrates the maximum number of consonants that can precede a vowel in English, which is three, and the maximum number that may follow a vowel, which is four (although there are five alphabetical consonants after the *e*, there are only four consonant phonemes, as we see in the transcription /strɛŋkθs/).

Perhaps the most difficult thing about syllables is not knowing what they are, but understanding where they begin and end. Let's think about the boundaries of a syllable.

Syllabification

Syllabification is the term for the division of a word into syllables and it is by no means a straightforward business. The word *working* clearly has two syllables. It consists of two morphemes, *work* + *ing*, so it is tempting to assume that syllabification corresponds to this morphological division. However, a phonetic division of the syllables gives *wor* + *king*. Similarly, the morphemes of *dirty* are *dirt* + *y* but phonetic syllabification is *dir* + *ty*. If you say the words *working* and *dirty* a few times, it is really not difficult to sense that the *k* of the former and the *t* of the latter are really the onsets of the second syllable. In transcriptions the convention is to use a central dot · to indicate the syllable divisions and the ' symbol to identify the stressed syllable, as in /saɪˈkɒl·ə·dʒɪst/ (*psychologist*).

Syllabic Consonants

Four different dictionaries give the following phonemic transcriptions for the word *beautiful*:

/ˈbjuːtɪˌfʊl/ (Oxford English Reference Dictionary)
/ˈbjuːtɪfl/ (Oxford Advanced Learner's Dictionary)
/ˈbjuːtəfl/ (Macmillan English Dictionary for Advanced Learners)
/ˈbjuːtɪfəl/ (Cambridge International Dictionary of English)

It is interesting, and perhaps somewhat comforting, to note that even professional lexicographers may have different perceptions of the standard RP production of a word. There is 100% agreement over the first syllable, which is unsurprising since it is the stressed syllable and stressed syllables are unambiguous. Unstressed syllables are more difficult to perceive and describe, and that explains why the *Macmillan Dictionary* transcribes the second syllable differently from the other three dictionaries. The main area of disagreement, however, concerns the *–ful* suffix of the third syllable. Words are not always pronounced in the same way; much depends on whether they are said in isolation or in the context of a longer utterance. The *Oxford English Reference Dictionary* transcribes the *–ful* suffix as it appears when an adjective is said in isolation and with particular care, while the other three focus on how it is said in speech of normal speed in the context of a typical communicative act. Even then there is some disparity: the *Cambridge International* uses a small schwa but the *Oxford Advanced* and the *Macmillan* do not. This does not mean, of course, that the teams of lexicographers who compiled the *Oxford Advanced* and the *Macmillan* are under the impression that the suffix at the end of *beautiful* is pronounced in the same way as the initial *fl* in *flower*. What it does mean, however, is that unstressed syllables composed of consonant + schwa + consonant are often delivered so quickly that the schwa is compressed to such a degree that the nucleus shifts from the vowel to the second consonant. This is the phenomenon of the *syllabic consonant*. So the appropriate phonemic transcription of *kettle* is not /ˈketəl/ but /ˈket·l/. In some dictionaries a small vertical line is placed under a syllabic consonant. Other words with the syllabic consonant *l* include /ˈpiː·pl/ (*people*), /ˈmɪd·l/ (*middle*) and /ˈhæg·l/ (*haggle*). The other consonants that sometimes become syllabic are *n*, as in /ˈfɪk·ʃn/ (*fiction*), and *r*, as in /ˈmɪs·tri/ (*mystery*). We may also find two syllabic consonants in sequence, as in /ˈræʃ·n·l/ (*rational*). Things are seldom clearcut, however, and for every dictionary that transcribes *rational* as /ˈræʃ·n·l/, there will be another that uses /ˈræʃ·n·əl/ or even /ˈræʃ·ən·əl/.

NECESSARY NOISES

Over to you 1

What words are represented by these transcriptions?

1 /ˈkɒn·trə·ˌvɜː·si/ 2 /kənˈtrɒv·ə·si/ 3 /ˌæl·jʊˈmɪn·ɪ·əm/ 4 /əˈluː·mɪ·nəm/

Check the *Key to Tasks* section.

Word Stress

Stress refers to the way a combination of volume, length and pitch can give prominence to a syllable. The vowels of unstressed or weak syllables tend to be shortened and centralised.

Polysyllabic words have a particularly prominent syllable that is said to have *primary stress*. Sometimes there is another fairly prominent syllable that has *secondary stress*. Note how the primary and secondary stresses are indicated in the transcription of *extermination*: /ɪkˌstɜːmɪˈneɪʃn/. The fourth syllable has primary stress. The second syllable has secondary stress and as a consequence its vowel is not reduced to schwa but remains long. The first syllable is unstressed and its vowel is not /e/ but the more centralised /ɪ/. The last syllable is weak and is reduced to a syllabic consonant (although it could also be transcribed with schwa).

Over to you 2

Transcribe these words indicating the primary stress with ' and, where it exists, the secondary stress with ˌ. Example: *communication* /kəˌmjuːnɪˈkeɪʃn/

1 contradiction 2 photographic 3 photographer 4 explanation
5 liberal 6 religious 7 hospital 8 curiosity

Now go to the *Key to Tasks* section.

Think about it 3

> Look at this conversational exchange. The word *that* appears three times. Think about how it would be pronounced in each case. You might also reflect upon the words *his*, *to*, *been* and *for*. Then consult the *Key to Tasks* section.
>
> "He said that he couldn't remember anything about his accident."
> "Well, he would say that. He doesn't want to tell us what happened or that he'd been drinking for two hours before he got in the car."

Bruisers and wimps in context

Many common words have a *full form* or a *strong form* when they are stressed and a *weak form* when they are unstressed. Typically, function words rather than content words are reduced to a weak form. These include determiners, pronouns, conjunctions, prepositions and auxiliary verbs. They are the kind of words that may sometimes be omitted from text messages without hindering comprehension. The preposition *at* is typically pronounced as /ət/ in a context such as *she was laughing at the story of our embarrassing experience*. If I want to contrast that preposition with another, however, I will draw attention to it by using the full form /æt/: *are you laughing with me or at me?* The position in the sentence is also important; the full form is more likely to occur at the beginning or at the end of a sentence. The weak form /kən/ appears in *she can speak three languages*, but the full form /kæn/ is used in the question *Can you speak German?* and in the short answer *Yes, I can*.

In the conversion from full to weak forms, vowels tend to shorten: /wɜː/ to /wə/ (*were*), /biːn/ to /bɪn/ (*been*). Both front and back vowels may centralise: /æz/ to /əz/ (*as*), /ɒv/ to /əv/ (*of*). Some consonants disappear: /ænd/ to /ən/ or even to a syllabic consonant (*and*), /mʌst/ to /məs/ (*must*). The initial /h/ in the words *he*, *him*, *his* and *her* disappears from the normal speed connected speech of all RP users, including those who are convinced that they are never guilty of the linguistic abomination of dropping their aitches.

NECESSARY NOISES

Over to you 3

Try to find words pronounced in both their weak and their full forms in the following utterances.

1. I don't know if Tim can speak Russian but I'm sure his sister can.
2. We're waiting for the bus. And you? What are you waiting for?
3. "Have you made many friends in this town?"
   "Not yet. I might have made more friends if I'd had a shorter working week."
4. Your name's Michael, I believe. But what's your surname?
5. We were totally lost. We had no idea where we were.
6. Must we really go to Angela's party? I don't like her friends at all. What's more, I must study for my exam tomorrow.
7. I want that one over there. Please don't tell me that you've promised it to someone else.
8. "What are you doing for your holiday this year? Are you going to Greece again?"
   "Yes, we are."
9. "She calls him her *boyfriend* but he's as old as her father."
   "As old! He's ten years older than her father!"
10. "You work for Bill, don't you?"
    "No, Bill's a colleague. I don't work for him but with him."

Now check the *Key to Exercises* section.

Stress and rhythm

Weak forms are important in establishing the alternation of strong and weak syllables in the rhythmic patterns of the English language. Some learners of English as a second language tend to give more or less the same prominence to all syllables, especially if their native language (Japanese or Spanish, for example) is one in which syllables are never weakened to the degree that they are in English. The result is a failure to imitate the appropriate rhythm, and this can cause the listener considerable strain. Even if the individual sounds are articulated well, the absence of the natural rhythm makes listening hard work, as you may know if you have tried to listen to a voice synthesiser for any length of time. In general it is probably true to say that both students and teachers of English should worry a little less about individual sounds and a little more about *suprasegmental features*, i.e. longer units of spoken language.

Poets, preachers and public speakers of all kinds know about the importance of rhythm. Much has been said and written about the metrical patterns of different kinds of poetry. Let's conclude the chapter with a reflection upon another kind of stress, that which disturbs the sleep of those who have great responsibility:

/ʌnˈiːzi ˈlaɪz ðə ˈhed ðət ˈweəz ə ˈkraʊn/

Now check the *Key to Tasks* section.

Chapter 5
JOINED-UP TALK

Think about it

"Take care of the sense, and the sounds will take care of themselves."
Lewis Carroll

Over to you 1

> Compose the longest sentence you can that consists entirely of monosyllabic words. Then go to the *Key to Tasks* section.

Assimilation

One way in which sounds influence one another is through *assimilation*, which means that a sound assumes some of the quality of a neighbouring sound, i.e. the two become similar in some way. For example, why is it that the *–ed* suffix on regular past tense verbs is sometimes pronounced as /t/ and sometimes as /d/? The answer is that it all depends on whether the preceding sound is voiced or unvoiced. Verbs that end with an unvoiced consonant, such as *hope* (/həʊp/), *like* (/laɪk/) and *miss* (/mɪs/), have the unvoiced /t/ in the *–ed* suffix: /həʊpt/, /laɪkt/, and /mɪst/. Verbs that end with a vowel or with a voiced consonant, such as *weigh* (/weɪ/), *call* (/kɔːl/) and *beg* (/beg/) have voiced /d/: /weɪd/, /kɔːld/ and /begd/. The same phenomenon is evident when we consider the quality of the final *–s* on the third person singular suffix, so we have unvoiced /s/ in /həʊps/ and /laɪks/ but voiced /z/ in /weɪz/ and /kɔːlz/. Similarly, the *–s* plural suffix is either /s/ or /z/ depending on the voiced or unvoiced quality of the final sound in the singular form of the noun.

The phenomenon described above is known as *progressive assimilation* because the presence or absence of voicing is carried forward to the next sound. In *regressive assimilation* an influence is carried in the opposite direction and often cuts across word boundaries. At one point in T.S. Eliot's *The Waste Land* the poet describes a group of working class friends leaving the pub and exchanging farewells through the repeated use of "goonight" (it appears six times in two lines). He then adds his own "good night" (three times in one line) as two separate words with all the consonants present and correct. With this juxtaposition of high and low registers, Eliot seeks to distinguish between the correct and incorrect diction of different social classes with very different educational backgrounds. However, as we have already seen with the substitution of /n/ for /ŋ/ in the *-ing* suffix, or the loss of initial /h/ in the weak forms of *his* and *her*, certain mutations dictated by linguistic context form part of the speech even of people who pride themselves on using "the Queen's English". In contracting *good night* to *goonight*, Eliot actually illustrates an example of assimilation that is certainly not restricted to working class people on their way out of the pub. Using the conventional alphabet he merely eliminates the final *d* of *good* to show what a phonemic transcription would render as /gʊn naɪt/, i.e. the initial /n/ of *night* convinces the plosive /d/ of *good* to undergo a radical conversion and become a nasal consonant the same as itself. That is not to say that we cannot say /gʊd naɪt/ if we wish to. It is largely a question of velocity; the faster and the less attentive we are, the greater the likelihood that /gʊn naɪt/ will emerge.

Regressive assimilation is far more likely when two fricatives bump up against each other. Try to say *close shave* quickly and it will soon become /kləʊʃ ʃeɪv/. If the initial *h* of *his shoes* is not aspirated we risk hearing one of the pronunciations of *issues* (which can be either /ˈɪʃuːz/ or /ˈɪsjuːz/). When two plosives meet the conversion may be partial; a rapid articulation of *nightgown* is likely to yield /ˈnaɪkgaʊn/, in which the /g/ causes the preceding alveolar consonant to become a velar consonant like itself, but the new /k/ retains an unvoiced inheritance from the original /t/.

Assimilation within a word may eventually lead to a permanent change in the standard pronunciation and orthography of a language. In modern Italian, for instance, we see that a process of assimilation has transformed the *ct* consonant cluster of Latin words such as *aspectus* (*aspect*) and *rectificare* (*rectify*) into *tt*, as in *aspetto* and *rettificare*.

Linking

In addition to influencing one another, our necessary noises also like joining together, and once again they do not respect word boundaries. As we have already seen with the expression *not at all*, final consonants tend to forge links with the initial vowels of subsequent words:

Dan_isn't_at_home now. Call_again_at_about_eight_o'clock.

Initial /h/ may disappear or become very faint to facilitate this linking:

I'll_ask_(H)arry to do it. It's_(h)is job.

We have said that in RP /r/ is only pronounced before a vowel, so when words like *for*, *our* and *their* stand in isolation the final /r/ is not pronounced. If these words precede a word that begins with a vowel, however, the /r/ appears and attaches itself to the vowel:

> There_isn't time to lose. After_all, we're_already late and our_only hope is to alter_all the plans before_Igor_arrives.

Some RP speakers bring in a linking /r/ even when no alphabetical *r* is present. This is called *intrusive r*, and it is not a feature of American English, or indeed of all RP speakers:

> Canada_/r/_isn't my idea_/r/_of a summer holiday destination.

If a word ends with /i/, for which the lips are somewhat spread, and the next word begins with a vowel, the link may be made with /j/:

> We_/j/_all had a lovely_/j/ _evening. The_/j/_Andersons were there and they_/j/_amused us with a story about their stay_/j/_in Argentina.

If a word ends with a vowel that requires rounded lips, the link is made with /w/:

> I know_/w/_all about it. You_/w/_ insisted that you didn't want to_/w/_eat anything but it was so_/w/_obvious that you_/w/_only said that to be polite. You'll
> do_/w/_ anything to_/w/_avoid appearing rude.

Having seen how spoken language often disregards word boundaries, it is legitimate to ask how it is that we can distinguish between *my trays* and *might raise*. This question of how we signal the demarcation between grammatical units is known as *juncture*. In this specific case we can note that final /t/ in a word like *might* is not aspirated, while many RP speakers aspirate initial /t/ in a word such as *trays*. This is an insufficient explanation, however, because some English speakers do not aspirate initial /t/, and in any case we have said that allophonic variation should not impact on meaning. A more important distinction concerns the /r/, which is voiced in initial position in *raise* but unvoiced after unvoiced /t/ in *trays*. The question of juncture is a complicated matter that goes far beyond the scope of a book such as this, but this one example demonstrates how the sounds "take care of themselves" to avoid the ambiguity that would otherwise compromise the speaker's sense.

Over to you 2

Try to identify the links in this passage, indicating linking /r/, /j/, or /w/ where necessary. Then go to the *Key to Tasks* section.

> My Aunt Agnes is an eccentric old lady. She's 73 and she says her ambition is to have her own helicopter. I think it's lucky that she isn't rich because if she had a lot of money to indulge her follies, she'd almost certainly waste it on silly ideas. But we all love old Agnes because she always knows how to make us laugh. Once I asked her why she had never married. "We single girls have more fun," she said. "We go out more and do all sorts of things. Anyway, I want to travel around and see something of the world before I marry and have kids." She was 68 at the time!

Elision

Elision is the technical term for the disappearance of sounds in certain contexts. Contracted forms are an example of elision, including the double contractions that one rarely sees in writing (*he'd've* for *he would have*, for example). Sounds are likely to be elided whenever the realisation of a full form is awkward or difficult. Consonant clusters can be difficult even for native speakers, and when speaking at normal speed many people use simplified forms and trust that their meaning will be made clear by context. The transition from a dental fricative to an alveolar fricative in *clothes* is difficult to articulate without slowing down and devoting particular attention, so the word is often reduced to *close* and no one interprets it as a synonym of *shut*. The plural forms of nouns that end with two consonants may also be simplified: /skrɪps/ for /skrɪpts/ (*scripts*), for example.

The final /t/ of words such as *must, just* and *can't* frequently disappears if the next word begins with a consonant:

1. I can'~~t~~ tell you yet. 2. You mus~~t~~ be joking. 3. I jus~~t~~ told him to go away.

Learners and teachers of English as a second language should not underestimate the importance of vowel length in the contracted form *can't* /kaːnt/. It is pronounced differently in Britain and in the USA but in both cases the vowel is long. Indeed, the fact that the final /t/ is frequently elided means that vowel length is actually the main indicator of negativity. Learners who do not lengthen the vowel sufficiently therefore risk uttering what listeners perceive as the affirmative /kæn/. Worse still, a vowel that is neither as long nor as far back as /ɑː/ plus a clearly articulated /t/ may result in a somewhat vulgar four-letter word.

Over to you 3

It's time to transcribe some joined-up talk. Think about how our necessary noises influence one another, forge links and sometimes disappear. Afterwards, check the *Key to Tasks* section.

1. She closed and locked the doors.
2. You just sit there for a few minutes.
3. Tell him to go away.
4. He isn't sure what his shares are worth.
5. You must be mad to even think about it.

Chapter 6
ATTITUDES AND FEELINGS

Think about it

What is this thing called love?
What is this thing called, love?
What? Is this thing called love?

If written words report *what* people said, it is punctuation that gives us indications as to *how* they said it, and how they said it depends on how they were feeling at the time. In the three questions above we have exactly the same words in exactly the same order but the meanings of the three utterances differ considerably. The title of Cole Porter's song suggests that someone is musing upon the ineffable mystery of romantic love. The insertion of a comma totally changes the sense of the question; it becomes a banal query about what an object is called, and *love* is no longer a sublime emotion but an affectionate term of address, usually for someone of the opposite sex. The third version does not lend itself to a standard interpretation but individual readers will doubtless be able to imagine a number of bizarre scenarios.

In spoken language we can communicate our attitudes and feelings – in ways that punctuation can never hope to replicate – through our use of *intonation*. Thus we supplement the meanings of the words we use with signals concerning our own moods and intentions as well as how we expect other people to receive our message. Entire volumes have been written on the subject of intonation and a short text such as this can do no more than introduce the essential principles.

Five basic tone patterns

The most frequently employed tone patterns are: falling (↘), rising (↗), level (→), rise-fall (↗↘) and fall-rise (↘↗).

The falling tone is associated with finality; the speaker has finished for the moment. This tone therefore has an important discoursal function related to the conventions of turn-taking since it indicates that the speaker has completed a contribution and someone else can now take a turn (although a truly emphatic falling tone can also suggest that the final word has been said and the topic is now closed). Declarative sentences and questions with an interrogative pronoun typically end with a falling tone, as do question tags that underline what has just been said rather than request confirmation.

The rising tone, in contrast, suggests incompletion. When we want to fend off an attempted interruption we raise our tone as well as volume to indicate that we haven't finished and have every intention of holding the floor for a while. The rising tone is, of course, the questioning tone; indeed, in some languages there are no syntactic indicators, such as subject-verb inversion, of the interrogative function, and tone is solely responsible for informing the interlocutor that an utterance is to be taken as a question. In English, yes/no questions (i.e. questions without an interrogative pronoun) end with a rising tone. A single word said with a rising tone can be a question (*Well?*), or even a sound that has no specific denotation (*Hmm?*). If we use a rising tone with an affirmative sentence there is again a sense of incompletion as we hint that there is a lot more to come if the interlocutor is interested in knowing more. Think about how the following statement might be intoned: *you'll never guess who I saw working at the massage parlour*. One can imagine the speaker saying this with a rising tone intended to prompt the interlocutor into giving a signal that s/he is willing to hear the gossip in all its detail.

It is no coincidence that the word *monotonous* is often used as a synonym for *boring* since the unchanging level tone is typical of routine verbal tasks that are inherently uninteresting, such as reading aloud a shopping list or calling a register of names. If a speech event is not boring in itself but one of the participants consistently uses a level tone we might interpret this as a sign of coldness, lack of cooperation or plain rudeness. A parent finds nothing boring about having to question an adolescent son or daughter about where s/he spent the night, but the young person's responses are often minimal, not only in terms of information imparted, but also as regards pitch range.

The rise-fall tone occurs in situations in which the written language might require an exclamation mark: when the speaker displays surprise or strong emotion, perhaps great joy, perhaps outrage.

Finally, we have the fall-rise tone that we sometimes hear when someone says *well* in a way that starts of apparently meaning *yes* but ends up implying *no, not really*. It can suggest scepticism, reluctant agreement or only partial agreement.

Well is a particularly useful word for studying the communicative functions of intonation because it is used in so many contexts, often with no real semantic value but merely as an indicator of the speaker's mood or attitude. Similarly, with the appropriate tone *hmm* can indicate reservation, curiosity, grumpiness and many other states of mind. Other useful monosyllables for observing the use of intonation are *yes* and *no*; we are all familiar with the emphatic *yes* that implies 'and don't you dare contradict me', the hesitant *yes* that is only too willing to be contradicted and the sarcastic *yes* that means 'no, not in a million years'.

ATTITUDES AND FEELINGS

Over to you 1

Concentrate on the words *yes* and *no* in these exchanges. Which of the five tones would you expect in each case? Afterwards go to the *Key to Tasks* section.

1. Are you ready?
   Yes. Start when you like.

2. Would you ever be unfaithful to me?
   No! How could you think such a thing.

3. Er... excuse me.
   Yes? Can I help you?

4. Have you ever had any of these illnesses? Glandular fever?
   No.
   Malaria?
   No.
   Gonorrhea?
   No! What do you take me for?

5. How about inviting Chris and Sandra to dinner on Friday?
   Yes. Although it means having their horrible kids here as well.

The Tone Unit and Tonic Syllables

Before proceeding with our phonological examination of intonation, we should briefly consider the phonetic description of the phenomenon. The following short text will be used for analysis:

> This is our philosophy. Our staff, from the managing director down to the tea-boy, have to show certain qualities. These include: honesty, respect for others, punctuality, and most of all, moral rectitude.

To consider how intonation operates, this text must be divided into *tone units* and the *tonic syllables* must be indicated. A tonic syllable is a stressed syllable that marks a significant shift in pitch. A tone unit is an utterance that contains one tonic syllable. There may be unstressed syllables before or after the tonic syllable, and the tone unit may contain other stressed syllables that do not coincide with a notable change in pitch. A tone unit can also consist of a tonic syllable and nothing else at all. If someone answers a question with a curt *yes*, that syllable is a tonic syllable that has a tone unit all to itself. Our text can be divided into eleven tone units as follows. Note that in this text stressed syllables other than the tonic syllables are not marked:

|| this is our phi◟losophy || our ◟╱staff || from the ╱<u>man</u>aging director || down to the ◟<u>tea</u>-boy || have to show certain ◟<u>qual</u>ities || these in◟╱<u>clude</u> || ╱<u>hon</u>esty || re╱<u>spect</u> for others || punctu╱<u>al</u>ity || and most of ╱<u>all</u> || moral ◟<u>rec</u>titude ||

A tone unit may be divided into the *head*, the *pre-head* and the *tail*. The head (H) runs from the first stressed syllable to the tonic syllable (TS). The pre-head (PH) is the part that precedes the first stressed syllable. The tail (T) is what follows the tonic syllable. In our text the second of the eleven tone units does not have a tail, several have a pre-head but no head and the seventh (the single word *honesty*) has neither head nor pre-head. The fifth tone unit includes all the divisions:

```
    PH          H           TS      T
|| have to | ,show ,certain | ◟qual | ities ||
```

Since the emphasis of this book is on phonology rather than phonetics, in the remainder of this chapter the consideration of how intonation operates in the English language will refer to the tone unit and the tonic syllable but not to the divisions of head, pre-head and tail.

Intonation and Grammar

So far we have noted that intonation gives us vital information about the speaker's feelings and attitudes. We have also seen that it is important in discourse in the negotiation of turn-taking, in hinting that the speaker has more to say or in sending out the message that there is nothing more to discuss (of course, intonation works in partnership with other factors, such as volume, facial expression and body language). We now need to look more closely at how intonation and grammar interact.

Something immediately striking about the short text used for analysis is the extent to which the eleven tone units coincide with syntactic boundaries.

ATTITUDES AND FEELINGS

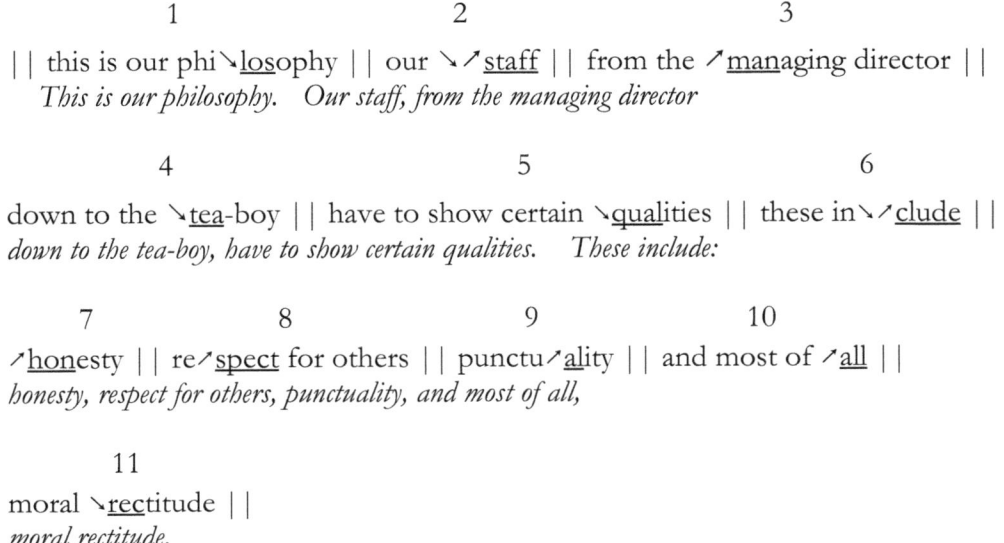

The first, fifth and eleventh tone units feature a falling tonic syllable and all three end at a point at which the written text has a full stop. As has already been noted, a falling tone tends to signal finality.

A rising tone suggests incompletion and the idea that there is more to follow, and in the list of qualities the speaker specifies, we find a sequence of rising tonic syllables in tone units that end where there is a comma in the written text. To show that the list has come to an end, there is a falling tonic syllable in the word *rectitude*. Lists have the ∕ ∕ ∕ ∕ ∖ sequence in texts such as this one in which the speaker displays enthusiasm, or at least, is not noticeably bored. If the speaker is not the least bit interested in the list s/he has to give, the pattern would, of course, be → → → → ∖.

The second tone unit features a fall-rise tonic syllable that signals the completion of a noun phrase but also announces the beginning of an utterance that is presented as two tone units, the first of which has a tonic syllable indicating incompletion and the second one that signals finality. Similarly, the fall-rise of the sixth tone unit signals the end of a verb phrase but announces the beginning of a list.

Going beyond this short text, it should also be noted that the tonic syllable has a key role in distinguishing between defining and non-defining clauses, and once again the tone units tend to correspond to syntactic boundaries. This time stressed syllables other than the tonic syllables are also marked:

My sister who lives in Australia is going to have a baby.
|| my ˌsister who ˌlives in Au∖∕stralia || is ˌgoing to ˌhave a ∖baby ||

My sister, who lives in Australia, is going to have a baby.
│ │ my ˋsister │ │ who ˌlives in Auˋ ˊstralia │ │ is ˌgoing to ˌhave a ˋbaby │ │

The sentence incorporating a defining clause is divided into two tone units. Although the first syllable of *sister* in the first tone unit is stressed, it does not carry tonic stress. The sentence containing a non-defining clause is divided into three tone units, each of which ends where a punctuation mark indicates a syntactic boundary in the written text. The first syllable of *sister* is now the tonic syllable of the first tone unit.

More on Intonation and Discourse

From the examples given above, it may be observed that the tonic syllable is often found in the last content word of a tone unit. There is no reason why it should not appear earlier, however. A key criterion concerns the "surprise factor" in the information we impart.

In typical discourse much of what we say is already partially known to our interlocutor because there is pre-existing *shared knowledge* or *common ground*. We all know about telephones, we know what they do, so in the first of the following utterances the tonic syllable is on the word *phone* rather than the verb that ends the tone unit. In the second utterance, in contrast, the phone does something unexpected, something that is not part of our shared knowledge of typical telephone behaviour, and the tonic syllable shifts accordingly.

The phone rang.   *The phone exploded.*
│ │ the ˋphone ˌrang │ │   │ │ the ˌphone ex ˋploded │ │

An excellent example is provided by Peter Roach (2001), who notes what happens with a routine activity involving a dog, and an activity that both dog and owner hope will not become routine:

I've got to take the dog for a walk.   *I've got to take the dog to the vet.*
│ │ Ive ˌgot to ˌtake the ˋdog for a ˌwalk │ │   │ │ Ive ˌgot to ˌtake the ˌdog to the ˋvet │ │

Some investigators in the field of intonation and discourse distinguish between *proclaiming tones*, with which the speaker's utterance adds something that is not already part of the common ground, and *referring tones*, which refer back to what is part of the shared knowledge of the participants. The falling tone is said to be the most common proclaiming tone, while fall-rise is the most typical referring tone. Adrian Underhill

(1998) gives the following example involving the discussion of a trip to towns in the south-east of England. The participants have already agreed that they will go to Hastings (shared knowledge) and the speaker now proposes a visit to Canterbury as well (an addition to the common ground). Note that Underhill's system of representing stress and tone has been adapted:

When we've visited Hastings, we'll go to Canterbury.
|| when weve ,visited ↘↗<u>hast</u>ings || well ,go to ↘<u>can</u>terbury ||

In the above example both the discourse and the grammatical functions of intonation are apparent: as regards the former, we note the fall-rise referring tone and the falling proclaiming tone, and for the latter we see that the two tone units correspond with the two clauses of the sentence.

Over to you 2

> Try to identify the tone units, the tonic syllables and the other stressed syllables in this sentence. Then check the *Key to Tasks* section.
>
> The first of April, which is the day for practical jokes, is our wedding anniversary.

Chapter 7
Right Watt Ewe Here

Think about it

> Rsearech ctundoced at an Elsgnih urvisuitey swohs taht it dseon't mtaetr waht odrer the lertets are in pvidored taht the frsit and lsat lttrees are wrhee tehy sohlud be. Tihs is baescue wehn we raed we dno't fucos on the idivdinaul lterets but on the wrod as a wlohe. Eevn if the ltreets bweteen the fsrit and the lsat are an asulbtoe mses we mganae to raed the txet awyany.

Why is English spelling so complicated?

For those who find the English spelling system a source of great frustration, it is perhaps reassuring to discover that even when the letters are as jumbled as they are in the text shown above, misspelt words are perfectly comprehensible. That does not mean, however, that we can be excessively tolerant of orthographical errors because it is not only Disgusted of Tunbridge Wells (whom we shall meet in the next chapter) who jumps to instant conclusions about people on the basis of whether or not they can spell properly; thousands of job applicants have had their CVs consigned unread to the wastepaper bin because in the accompanying letter they had spelt *accommodation* with only one *m*. The crux of the problem is, of course, the mismatch between pronunciation and spelling, and it is worth taking a look at the historical reasons for this situation.

Until the late 15th century there was no standardised system of spelling for the English language, and texts written in Middle English (i.e. the English between the 11th and the 14th centuries when the Germanic language of Old English came to be lexically and grammatically influenced by French and Latin) often feature variations upon a word that reflect regional pronunciation and the intuitions of individual writers. Compared to the English of today, however, there was a far greater correlation between pronunciation and spelling. Standardisation owes much to William Caxton who, having learnt the technique of mechanical printing in Cologne and Bruges, set up his own printing press in London in 1476. The new technology required a standardised system of spelling and Caxton was faced with the impossible task of trying to please everyone at a time when there was not even a consensus as to the variety of English to be taken as a model. He made his (often idiosyncratic) decisions as to how words were to be spelt, and although standardisation did not occur overnight, he triggered a process that was to prove to be inexorable.

NECESSARY NOISES

Mechanical printing gave an enormous boost to publishing and the diffusion of knowledge, but as far as the link between pronunciation and spelling was concerned, it came a century too early. When Caxton set up his printing press, another, equally unstoppable, process was already under way and would go on to revolutionise the sound system of English by the end of the 16th century (though it continued to exert an influence right up until the 18th century): the Great Vowel Shift (GVS). For reasons that researchers are still investigating, the vowels of English, particularly the long vowels, underwent gradual but ultimately radical changes. The problem was that by the time the GVS had run its course, the orthography of English had already been standardised according to a pre-GVS system that no longer represented the pronunciation of the language. To take just one example, in many common words the open, back vowel /ɑː/ first shifted forward to long, front /aː/, then became closer, but still long, as /eː/, and finally settled as the diphthong /eɪ/. So today we use that diphthong to pronounce as /neɪm/ the word we write as *name*, the spelling of which is more appropriate to its pre-GVS pronunciation, which was /nɑːm/. And pronunciation and spelling have remained out of sync ever since.

Another important factor has been the lexicographical tradition of prescribing spellings that acknowledge the etymology of words, often by the insertion of letters that are not pronounced. Thus the silent *b* of *debt* acknowledges its Latin origin in *debitum*, the *h* of *chaos* relates to the Greek *khaos* and the *w* of *sword* is inherited from Old English *sweord* and Old High German *swert*.

There have been various attempts at spelling reform, none of which have enjoyed conspicuous success. A major obstacle to the establishment of a phonetic system of spelling is the existence of so many *homophones*, i.e. pairs of words that sound the same but have different spellings and meanings. A phonemic transcription of the title of this chapter would be /raɪt wɒt juː hɪə/, a sequence of sounds that could also represent the words "write what you hear". There is an extraordinary number of homophones in English: *cell/sell, rain/reign/rein, site/sight/cite, days/daze, allowed/aloud, source/sauce, weather/whether, court/caught, sun/son, would/wood, chews/choose, great/grate* etc., and a more "rational" spelling system would necessitate the essentially irrational measure of adopting the same orthographic form for two or even three quite distinct lexemes. The written language would be extremely ambiguous if we had a single spelling for three such commonly used words as *to*, *two* and *too*. The fact is that we are stuck with the spelling system that we've got. It is not fixed for all eternity – it is in the nature of a living language to change over time – but modifications will occur gradually and certainly not in response to any clumsy attempt at "linguistic engineering"

Since we have to live with English spelling as it is, it is not a bad idea to find out something about how it works as a system. It is a system, and not an anarchic free-for-all as some would maintain, but its rules may not be immediately evident.

The remainder of this chapter is concerned with practical tips on how to relate the writing system to the sound system.

Over to you 1

> This task should be easy for native speakers but non-native speakers may have a few difficulties. The following "words" do not really exist (unless they are obscure archaic or technical terms unknown to the author). How would you pronounce them?
>
> 1. fep   2. fepe   3. wibe   4. wib   5. muction   6. mution   7. klabious   8. phabbious

Check your suggested pronunciations in the *Key to Tasks* section.

Examples 1 – 4 above exemplify a rule governing the pronunciation of vowels. Now look at the pairs of words in the task below and try to work out what it is.

Over to you 2

> What is the effect of adding *e* to these three-letter (in one case two-letter) words?
>
> hat-hate   sit-site   hop-hope   tun-tune   pet-Pete
> rap-rape   rip-ripe   con-cone   us-use   bed-Bede
>
> Check the *Key to Tasks* section.

Over to you 3

> What do you note about the pronunciation of these words?
>
> completion   relation   solution   motion
> congestion   reaction   function   option
>
> Go to the *Key to Tasks* section

Another rule concerning the pronunciation of vowels has already been covered: *r* lengthens the preceding vowel (*ham* vs *harm*, *fen* vs *fern*, *fist* vs *first*, *pot* vs *port*, *bust* vs *burst*). We have also seen how a stress shift can distinguish verbs from nouns: the stress is on the first syllable in the nouns *desert* (/ˈdezət/), *insult* (/ˈɪnsʌlt/) and *produce* (/ˈprɒdjuːs/) while the verbs that are spelt in the same way have the stress on the second syllable (/dɪˈzɜːt/, /ɪnˈsʌlt/ and /preˈdjuːs/). It should be added that the same stress shift can also differentiate between adjectives and verbs, with adjectives taking first syllable stress. Thus *perfect* as an adjective is pronounced /ˈpɜːfɪkt/ but as a verb it becomes /pəˈfekt/.

There was no equivalent of the Great Vowel Shift for consonants, and today the correlation between spelling and pronunciation is more reliable for consonant letters. One potentially problematic letter is *c*, which is sometimes pronounced as /k/ and sometimes as /s/. The rule is that it is /s/ before *i* (*city*), *e* (*centre*) and *y* (*cynic*) but /k/ before all other vowels and also before consonants. The same pattern is applicable to the /dʒ/ and /g/ pronunciations of *g*, although in this case a number of very common words are exceptions to the rule: *get*, *give*, *girl* and *anger*.

Whether *ch* is pronounced as the affricate /tʃ/ or the plosive /k/ is largely a question of etymology; it is /k/ in words derived from Greek, such as *chorus* (from *khoros*), *technology* (from *tekhnologia*) and *schism* (from *skhisma*). It may also be pronounced /ʃ/ in words of French origin, such as *louche*.

When two symbols are combined to function as a single element, such as *ch*, it is known as a *digraph*. With some English digraphs the first component is not pronounced; when the digraphs *kn*, *gn*, *ps* and *pn* occur in initial position, only the *n* or *s* components are pronounced. Examples include the words *knight*, *know*, *gnome*, *psychology* and *pneumatic*. In final position the second component of the *mb* digraph is silent (*bomb*, *thumb*, *tomb*). The *b* remains silent in medial position if *mb* is a digraph, but not, of course, if *m* and *b* function as separate consonants (compare *bomber* /ˈbɒmə/ and *number* /ˈnʌmbə/).

There is, it seems, some method in the apparent madness of English spelling and pronunciation. That said, it can be demoralising to learn that –*ough* is pronounced /əʊ/ in *although*, /ə/ in *thorough*, /uː/ in *through*, /ɔː/ in *bought*, /aʊ/ in *plough*, /ʌf/ in *rough*, /ɒf/ in *cough* and /ʌp/ in *hiccough*.

Over to you 4

The Dutch teacher and writer, Gerald Nolst Trenité, who wrote under the pseudonym *Charivarius*, wrote a poem called *The Chaos* in which he made fun of English spelling. The full poem is 275 lines long and some of the vocabulary seems rather obscure to the modern reader, but it is still a very clever work with an extraordinary range of examples of "chaotic" spelling. Here are the first eight lines. Try to write a phonemic transcription of it, then check the *Key to Tasks* section. In transcribing poetry you can use the full forms of all syllables.

Dearest creature in creation,
Study English pronunciation.
I will teach you in my verse
Sounds like corpse, corps, horse, and worse.
I will keep you, Susy, busy,
Make your head with heat grow dizzy.
Tear in eye, your dress will tear.
So shall I! Oh hear my prayer.
Charivarius (Gerald Nolst Trenité)

Chapter 8
DISGUSTED OF TUNBRIDGE WELLS

Tunbridge Wells in the south-east of England is actually rather a nice town with a high standard of living, low unemployment and, by British standards, a pleasant climate. One of the very few bad things to say about the place is that it is the home of a certain "Disgusted". That is not his real name, of course, but the pseudonym he adopts every time he fires off one of his angry letters to the editor of the local newspaper (he must surely have a thoroughly sensible name like William or Charles, for the current fashion of giving children exotic names is one of the many things he cannot stand). His letters cover a range of subjects – the lack of manners nowadays, disgraceful public services, the calamitous decline in moral standards – but a single, overriding theme links them all: the country is going to the dogs. At a moment's notice he can produce a mixed salad of metaphors to warn of our imminent descent into a far greater chaos than Gerald Nolst Trenité ever envisaged: this is the thin edge of the wedge as we stumble blindly forward on the slippery slope along the thorny path and down the blind alley leading to the loss of our cherished freedoms and the end of civilisation as we know it. Among the things he considers particularly harmful to the future well-being of the United Kingdom, we can list: young people, comprehensive schools, men with ear-rings, women with tattoos, young people, all music composed after 1955, swearing on TV, mobile phones, speed cameras and young people.

Nothing infuriates Disgusted of Tunbridge Wells quite as much as the gratuitous violence inflicted upon our proud and beautiful language, for he does not see English as a set of necessary noises but as a great gift bequeathed to us by the giants of literature, a gift that we must treasure and defend. Flogging is too good for those who say *cheers* instead of *thankyou*. The abomination of putting a preposition at the end of a sentence threatens to undermine our society, something that he never tires of warning us about. The dropping of aitches is an open invitation to the four horsemen of the Apocalypse according to Disgusted, whose every syllable from the moment he began to opine his first disgusted gurgles has been full and perfectly articulated. People who split infinitives should have molten lead poured in their ears, and Disgusted would be happy to personally supervise the pouring. Disgusted, you see, believes in linguistic *prescriptivism*, the view that an official version of correct usage should be decided by people who have the necessary authority and knowledge, and the rest of us should stick religiously to the rules. Modern linguists take a rather different view, but Disgusted has little time for linguists; on his list of untrustworthy types they occupy a position just above sociologists and just below young people.

But living languages do not stand still, and however many angry letters Disgusted writes, the sound of English will change over time. When British people hear old newsreels from the 1940s and 50s they cannot help but notice something a bit odd about the RP of half a century ago. The /æ/ vowel, for instance, appears to be more open today, closer to /a/, for the BBC newsreaders of the 1940s seem to say *men* for *man*. We will now look at two current developments in the sound system of English, one involving English as a global language, the other specific to British English.

High-Rise Terminals

We noted in chapter 6 that a falling tone suggests finality and is therefore used in affirmative sentences while a rising tone indicates incompletion and is most commonly used in interrogatives. That is the conventional wisdom but a phenomenon that many have noted in the last two decades is that of *high-rise terminals*, the use of a rising tone at the end of statements. It is a development that has occupied teachers and journalists quite as much as linguists, and is generally referred to in the media by the less technical term *uptalk*. Users of uptalk make every utterance sound like a question, to Disgusted a sure sign that Armageddon lies just around the corner.

There has been considerable debate but absolutely no agreement concerning the origins of uptalk. One theory is that, like so many new trends, it began with young people on the west coast of the United States, spread eastwards, then reached the United Kingdom via TV and films. However, this explanation does not account for the fact that a prominent uptalker is the archetypal New Yorker Woody Allen, who was born in 1935. It is even less convincing as an explanation for the appearance of high-rise terminals in the speech of British people since all the evidence suggests that while TV may have an effect on our vocabulary, particularly through the diffusion of American slang, it does not significantly influence phonological features. Two generations of British people have grown up with substantial weekly exposure to televised American English and there has not been a discernible influence on their pronunciation. For the transfer of phonological characteristics interaction is necessary, for it is only through conversation that the phenomenon of *accommodation* (when one speaker unconsciously adjusts his/her speech to match that of an interlocutor) can occur.

For similar reasons, we can also discount the theory that British children imitated the high-rise terminals they heard on the Australian soap operas that began to be screened on television in the UK from the late 1980s. That said, it should be noted that Australian linguists began to report on the phenomenon some twenty-five years ago.

A third theory traces the origin of uptalk to Ireland, and its diffusion to the fact that great numbers of Irish emigrants have settled in the USA, the UK, Australia and New Zealand, i.e. in countries in which high-rise terminals are now evident. This would explain why the presence of uptalk has not been reported in the Indian subcontinent or anglophone Africa where there has not been an Irish influx. It is difficult, however, to see why this alleged influence of Irish intonation did not become apparent much earlier given that Irish people have been leaving their homeland for more than two centuries. Indeed, the emergence of uptalk has occurred in precisely the period in which the success of the Celtic tiger economy has meant that Ireland's brightest no longer need to seek their fortunes abroad.

If there is no consensus concerning the origin of uptalk, neither is there agreement regarding its significance. One view is that the rising, questioning tone is symptomatic of a society that is unsure of itself and of a generation of young people who are reluctant to commit themselves to firm statements or the declaration of absolute truths. Thus the rising tone is a kind of hedging mechanism by which the speaker seeks confirmation that the interlocutor approves of what has been said, and simultaneously signals a willingness to accept correction or contradiction. It has even been suggested that the inherent insecurity of the job market in post-industrial society is linked to an apparent lack of self-confidence indicated by high-rise terminals. Further support for the link between a sense of insecurity and a rising tone has come from researchers who claim that uptalk is more prevalent among females than males (though there is no consensus here either). The theory is that despite the advances made by the feminist movement, women still tend to be less assertive than men and their use of high-rise terminals shows that they continue to seek men's approval.

A very different theory postulates that far from signalling insecurity, in uptalk the rising tone is used with its function of indicating incompletion, the fact that the speaker has more to say. In chapter 6 we saw that raising tone along with volume is a way of fending off an attempted interruption; it could be, therefore, that the use of uptalk is a kind of pre-emptive strike, a way of blocking the interruption before it is even made. If that is the case, high-rise terminals suggest a desire to hold the floor for an extended contribution, which is more indicative of high self-confidence than the contrary.

Whatever its origins and whatever its significance, uptalk is a reality and it is not a phenomenon exclusive to young people. I can think of at least two people in late middle-age whom I have known for many years who have recently started using high-rise terminals (for Disgusted of Tunbridge Wells it is particularly galling when people old enough to know better ape the mannerisms of the young). The diffusion of uptalk is a work in progress and we cannot predict how far it will go, but it is conceivable that we will have to revise our idea of how intonation works in the phonological model we teach learners of English. Indeed, we may even have to think the unthinkable and call into question the appropriateness of Received Pronunciation as a model for learners to imitate.

Think about it

> Only about 3% of the British population speak RP and although it remains the prestige variety, there is more and more acceptance of regional pronunciations in all walks of life. If you are not a native speaker of English, do you still want RP to be your pronunciation model? How do/would you feel about having lessons with an English teacher who speaks/spoke a regional accent? If you are a native speaker of English, do you think RP speakers still enjoy certain advantages in British society? What alternative pronunciation model(s) could we adopt? Do all British regional accents have the same level of acceptance or are some "more equal than others"?

Estuary English: a challenge to RP?

When Alf Ramsey became coach of the England football team in 1963 he had elocution lessons in order to aquire RP because he felt that his new position was incompatible with his native Cockney accent. Today it is not at all unusual to find senior administrators, academics, high court judges and – something that was once inconceivable – BBC presenters who have retained a mild form of their regional accent. Not only is a non-RP variety no longer the professional handicap it once was, but the traditional voice of the Establishment has also been criticised for being socially divisive. It has the great advantage of not being associated with any particular region, but it does not have the same neutrality in terms of social class. While there will always be a need for a widely accepted pronunciation model, not everyone is convinced that a variety spoken by such a small, and often privileged, minority is really the most appropriate social dialect to adopt.

The expression *Estuary English* first appeared as the title of an article by David Rosewarne published in the Times Educational Supplement in October 1984. The estuary in question is that of the Thames, the river that flows through London, and the accent of the capital city (Cockney) is one of the two components involved in the emergence of Estuary English (EE). The other one is RP. As Rosewarne puts it, 'If one imagines a continuum with RP and London speech at either end, "Estuary English" speakers are found to be grouped in the middle ground.' The expression Estuary English quickly gained general acceptance and the phenomenon has now been studied in considerable detail. One of the more controversial claims in Rosewarne's original article is his assertion that for 'large and influential sections of the young, the new model for general imitation may already be "Estuary English", which may become the RP of the future.' For a linguistic variety to become the model for an entire population, powerful social forces are required.

The term Cockney refers not only to an accent but also to a dialect that features departures from standard grammar. Two examples of non-standard grammar are the substitution of the past participle *done* for the preterite *did* and the omission of the *–ly* suffix on adverbs, which results in the observation of another former coach of the England football team (who did not have elocution lessons) that 'the boy done brilliant there'. EE refers only to accent and is in no way associated with non-standard use of grammar and lexis. Since it sits somewhere on a continuum, it is obvious that some EE speakers will be closer to the Cockney pole and others closer to the RP end, so clear boundaries do not exist. We can, however, note that EE adopts some of the characteristics of Cockney but not others, and this selectivity is essential if it is ever to acquire the prestige of a model.

J.K. Rowling's latest blockbuster is entitled *Harry Potter and the Deathly Hallows*, which an authentic Cockney would pronounce as /ˈæri ˈpɒʔə rən ðə ˈdefli ˈæləʊz/. As we have already seen, all English speakers drop initial /h/ in weak forms but a characteristic of Cockney is the loss of aspiration also in full forms in stressed words such as *Harry* and *hallows*. It is a stigmatised feature of London speech, something unfairly associated with ignorance, and people who consider themselves speakers of correct English place great importance on never dropping their aitches. The loss of initial /h/ in stressed syllables is not typical of EE.

The *deathly* of the book title is rendered as /ˈdefli/ in Cockney. Another characteristic of the London dialect is the substitution of the labiodental fricatives /f/ and /v/ for the linguodental /θ/ and /ð/ (*fing* for *thing*, *bruvver* for *brother*), and this is also a feature that people from outside London try to avoid. Once again, EE's candidature as the RP of the future is favoured by its rejection of this somewhat below-stairs aspect of Cockney.

The transcription of *Harry Potter and the Deathly Hallows* includes a new symbol (/ʔ/), which stands for what is known as the *glottal plosive*, or more commonly but less accurately, the *glottal stop* (like all plosives it is a stop followed by a release). It is produced when the vocal cords are shut tightly, then suddenly opened to release air through the glottis. In Cockney, and indeed in several other dialects of English, the glottal plosive may replace /t/ in medial or final positions, so a Londoner might pronounce *what a lot of water* as /wɒʔ ə lɒʔ ə wɔːʔə/. Because it nearly always replaces /t/ and its use does not alter meaning, many phonologists consider /ʔ/ to be an allophone of /t/ in English rather than a phoneme in its own right. In EE the glottal plosive is not ubiquitous as it is in Cockney but it is used, especially in final position in words such as *went* (/wenʔ/) or *wrote* (/rəʊʔ/). An EE speaker would be most unlikely to use /ʔ/ in medial position between vowels as in the Cockney realisation of *water*, but (s)he might well use it after a consonant in a word like *saunter*. Like the dropped /h/ in unstressed syllables, the glottal plosive is something that many people use without being aware of the fact; indeed, they might protest most strongly that they always pronounce a distinct /t/. Use of /ʔ/ is clearly on the increase, however, and this appears to be a development to support the claim that EE is the RP of the future.

It is sometimes said that a true Cockney must be born within the sound of Bow bells, that is, near enough to St Mary-le-Bow church in the area known as Cheapside to hear the tolling of the church bells. And another sign of a true Cockney is that when s/he says *bow* and *bell* the final sounds of both words are very similar. It is the *l* of *bell* that sounds like the *w* of *bow* rather than vice versa; similarly, the *l* of *felt* or *milk* also sounds like a *w* in London English. In phonetic terms the phenomenon is described as the vocalisation of final and preconsonantal dark *l*, and it is an aspect of Cockney that most definitely forms part of the phonological behaviour of Estuary English. An EE speaker might produce the following:

Tell Phil I've sold the gold belt
/teʊ fɪʊ aɪv soʊd ðə goʊd beʊt/

So EE incorporates such Cockney characteristics as the use of the glottal plosive or the vocalisation of dark *l* but eschews more socially stigmatised features like dropped /h/ or failure to produce the phonemes represented in written English by *th*. Judicious selection of this kind is necessary if EE is ever going to challenge RP as the pronunciation model of British English. An important factor in its favour is that there are more speakers of EE than of RP, and the numerical gap seems destined to widen given that fewer and fewer people feel the need to acquire RP in adulthood to improve their career prospects. Indeed, the fact that RP is associated with the privileged social classes actually deters some individuals from wishing to imitate it.

The major weakness of EE as a potential model is evident in its name: it is still a localised variety, while RP, in contrast, has speakers who were born in Sheffield, Edinburgh, Swansea or Belfast. The heartland of EE is in London and the south-east of England, and although its influence is spreading over an ever wider geographical area (it has reached Tunbridge Wells by now, much to the distaste of one of its residents), it is difficult to imagine the day when mothers in Newcastle or Glasgow will scold their children for having /spɪʊt/ their /mɪʊk/. It is impossible to predict how far or how quickly EE will spread north and west. Only time will tell, or /wɪʊ teʊ/.

The final word

If Disgusted of Tunbridge Wells had been around in the 15th century he would doubtless have worn out several quills protesting in the strongest possible terms about the Great Vowel Shift, and a lot of good it would have done him. Major phonetic changes have a life of their own and there is little we can do to stop them. It is too early to say if uptalk is here to stay, or whether Estuary English will one day conquer the whole of the United Kingdom, but no amount of prescriptivism will either hasten or reverse events.

     Phonology is often seen as a rather dry subject of little immediate relevance to everyday life. The aim of this little book has been to counter that impression and show that the necessary noises that distinguish us from other animals are well worth studying. They are noises that keep evolving and mutating. The reader now has, I hope, the essential tools necessary to understand those changes a little better.

KEY TO TASKS

Chapter 1: Think about it

Several researchers in the fields of First and Second Language Acquisition have found evidence to support the Critical Period Hypothesis, which states that up to a certain age a child can acquire a second language easily and achieve native-speaker competence. After that critical period the process becomes more difficult and the learner's second language (L2) usually fossilises somewhere short of native-speaker competence. The end of the critical period is often put at puberty, but for pronunciation some investigators believe that the key age is much earlier, even as young as six years, because the articulators of speech quickly lose flexibility.

Native-speaker pronunciation is not a realistic target for most learners, and many people are not at all concerned about continuing to "sound foreign". Others wish to improve their L2 pronunciation but are frustrated by their inability to do so. When it comes to grammar and vocabulary, learners often feel that it is in their power to work hard and improve their level, and can accept that failure is to a considerable extent their own fault. For pronunciation there is not necessarily the same correspondence between effort exerted and results achieved.

A rule of thumb for teachers is whether the student's pronunciation creates strain for the listener. An obviously foreign accent that is nevertheless easy to understand is no great problem, but if sustained effort is required to make sense of what someone is saying, the obvious risk is that the listener will get bored or irritated and then switch off. Pronunciation practice in the classroom must be handled with tact and sensitivity, however, for some adult learners might feel that they can no more pronounce *th* than they can change the colour of their eyes or grow taller, and that being nagged to do what they patently cannot do is merely an exercise in humiliation. Rather than focus on individual sounds – tormenting hapless Japanese students with the "red lorry yellow lorry" conundrum – teachers might do better to work on larger units, especially intonation patterns (Chapter 6). Appropriate intonation can partially compensate for poorly articulated individual sounds.

NECESSARY NOISES

Chapter 2: Over to you

The Consonant Phonemes of Received Pronunciation

	Bilabial	Labiodental	Linguo-dental	Alveolar	Palato-alveolar	Palatal	Velar	Glottal
Fricative		f v	θ ð	s z	ʃ ʒ			h
Plosive	p b			t d			k g	
Affricate					tʃ dʒ			
Nasal	m			n			ŋ	
Lateral				l				
Approximant	w			r		j		

Chapter 3: Over to you 1

In Chapter 2 we noted that an important difference between RP and American English is that in the former /r/ is only pronounced before a vowel while in the latter it also occurs before a pause and before a consonant. But in RP even when the letter *r* is not pronounced it has the important phonological function of lengthening the preceding vowel. *Sharm* and *thork* are invented words and therefore have no recognised pronunciation but the presence of post-vocalic *r* would induce most readers to say them as /ʃaːm/ and /θɔːk/.

The "partnership" between /r/ and /l/ is again evident, for the latter sometimes follows one of the long vowels: *alms, balm(y), calm, half, psalm*.

Chapter 3: Over to you 2

1. church 2. fox 3. lose 4. health 5. yellow 6. ring 7. cut 8. those 9. cry 10. jaw

Chapter 3: Over to you 3

1. /nɪə/ 2. /saɪz/ 3. /bʌtə/ 4. /lʊk/ 5. /θɜːti/ 6. /niːd/ 7. /heə/ 8. /rɑːðə/ 9. /ɜːli/ 10. /wɒʃ/

Chapter 4: Think about it 2

Present, *perfect* and *rebel* are bisyllabic words. When they are used as nouns (or as an adjective in the case of *perfect*) the first syllable is the strong, stressed syllable and the second is weak and unstressed. When they are converted into verbs, however, the wimpish second syllables become bruisers to be reckoned with, and it is the first syllables that get sand kicked in their faces. Shifting the stress also has an effect on the quality of the syllables concerned, particularly the nature of the vowel sounds. As a noun *rebel* is pronounced /ˈrebl/ but as a verb it is /rɪˈbel/. This will be investigated later in the chapter.

    Other words that undergo a shift in stress when they change word class from noun to verb include *conduct, contract, contrast, desert, export, import, insult, object, produce, protest, record* and *subject*.

Chapter 4: Over to you 1

Numbers 1 and 2 are two pronunciations of the word *controversy*, the former with the stress on the first syllable and the latter with the stress on the second. Note how moving the stress affects the vowels /ɒ/ and /ə/. In addition to the *primary stress* (indicated by ˈ), in number 1 the *secondary stress* (ˌ) is also indicated, and this has an influence on the vowels /ɜː/ and /ə/.

    Number 3 is the RP pronunciation of *aluminium* and Number 4 is the American pronunciation of the same word. Once again the placement of stress affects the quality and length of vowels.

Chapter 4: Over to you 2

1 /ˌkɒntrəˈdɪkʃn/   2 /ˌfəʊtəˈɡræfɪk/   3 /fəˈtɒɡrəfə/   4 /ˌəkspləˈneɪʃn/
5 /ˈlɪbrl/ or /ˈlɪbərəl/   6 /rɪˈlɪdʒəs/   7 /ˈhɒspɪtl/   8 /ˌkjʊərɪˈɒsɪti/

Chapter 4: Think about it 3

The word *that* can be a conjunction, a relative pronoun, a determiner or a demonstrative pronoun and its pronunciation varies according to its role and importance in an utterance. It has a *full form* /ðæt/ and a *weak form* /ðət/. The first time *that* appears in the conversation it is a conjunction introducing a reporting clause and it would be possible to omit it. Given its limited importance it is not stressed and is therefore pronounced as /ðət/. The second time *that* appears it is much more important because it substitutes for the accident victim's entire assertion that he cannot remember anything, so this time it is pronounced with its full form /ðæt/. Then it is used a third time, again to introduce a reporting clause, and the weak form is natural.

Other weak forms can be identified. After the final alveolar plosive of *about*, in conversation at normal speed *his* is likely to be produced in its weak form /ɪz/ rather than its full form /hɪz/. The *to* of *want to tell* has the weak form /tʊ/ or /tə/ and not the full form /tuː/. In the present perfect continuous the past participle *been* is typically shortened from the full form /biːn/ to the weak form /bɪn/. Finally, the preposition *for* has a long vowel in its full form /fɔː/ but is shortened to /fə/ in its weak form.

KEY TO TASKS

Chapter 4: Over to you 3

1. I don't know if Tim /kən/ speak Russian but I'm sure his sister /kæn/.
   In final position the full form of *can* is used.

2. We're waiting /fə/ the bus. And /juː/? What are /jʊ/ waiting /fɔː/?
   Shortening of vowels in weak forms from /ɔː/ to /ə/, and from /uː/ to /ʊ/.

3. "/hæv/ you made many friends in this town?"
   "Not yet. I might /əv/ made more friends if I'd had a shorter working week."
   Full form at start of sentence. Weak form with loss of aspiration after modal verb.

4. /jɔː/ name's Michael, I believe. But what's /jə/ surname?
   Full form with long vowel at start of sentence.

5. We /wə/ totally lost. We had no idea where we /wɜː/.
   Full form with long vowel at end of sentence.

6. /mʌst/ we really go to Angela's party? I don't like /ə/ friends at all. What's more, I /məs/ study /fə/ my exam tomorrow.
   Before a consonant, final *t* of weak form of *must* is dropped. Weak forms of *her* and *for*.

7. I want /ðæt/ one over there. Please don't tell me /ðət/ you've promised it to someone else.
   Full form has the important function of identifying something; weak form is a conjunction that could be omitted.

8. "What /ə/ you doing for /jə/ holiday this year? /ɑː/ you going to Greece again?"
   "Yes, we /ɑː/."
   Full forms at beginning and end of sentence.

9. "She calls him her *boyfriend* but he's /əz/ old /əz/ her father."
   "/æz/ old! He's ten years older /ðən/ her father!"
   The second speaker consciously highlights the word *as* and uses the full form.

10. "You work /fə/ Bill, don't you?"
    "No, Bill's a colleague. I don't work /fɔː/ him but with him."
    Prepositions are usually weak but for contrastive purposes the second speaker highlights *for*.

Chapter 4: Stress and rhythm

/ʌnˈiːzi ˈlaɪz ðə ˈhed ðət ˈweəz ə ˈkraʊn/

"Uneasy lies the head that wears a crown" from Shakespeare's *Henry IV Part 2*, Act III, Scene I.
This is an example of iambic pentameter, i.e. a ten-syllable line with a regular weak-strong-weak-strong pattern throughout. Three of the weak syllables have schwa, a fourth has the short, central vowel /ʌ/ and a fifth has /i/, which is somewhere between long and short. Of the five stressed syllables, three have a diphthong and one has the long vowel /iː/.

Chapter 5: Over to you 1

A characteristic of the English language is that an extraordinary number of the most frequently used words are monosyllabic. It is really not particularly difficult to put together in a meaningful sentence a sequence of 30 one-syllable words. If we were to pronounce each word as a separate entity, the language would have a kind of "staccato" quality rather than a rhythmic flow. In practice, when all these short words rub shoulders they influence one another, find ways to form links and do whatever they have to do to live together harmoniously. The white space that separates one word from the next on the written page often bears little relation to the position of pauses in spoken delivery. Think about how we say *Not at all, mate*. Is there any discernible difference between that and *Not a tall mate*? (in the second utterance *tall* would probably carry greater stress than the *all* of the first utterance but the difference is not easy to perceive). Someone studying English as a second language might search in vain in the dictionary to find out what a *notatorl* is. Word boundaries do not always coincide with the boundaries between sounds. We do not think about such things when we talk because we are concerned with conveying meaning, and we take it for granted that the sounds will adapt to our purposes. And they do; while people take care of the sense, our necessary noises take care of themselves.

KEY TO TASKS

Chapter 5: Over to you 2

My_Aunt_Agnes_is_an_eccentric_old lady. She's_73_ /j/_and she says_(h)er_ambition_is to have her_own helicopter. I_think_it's lucky that she_/j/_isn't_rich because_if she had_a_lot_of money to_/w/_indulge_(h)er follies, she'd_almost certainly waste_it_on silly_ideas. But we_ /j/_all love_old Agnes because she_ /j/_always knows how to make_us laugh. Once_I_ /j/_asked_(h)er why she had never married. "We single girls_(h)ave more fun," she said. "We go_ /w/_out more and do_/w/_all sorts_of things. Anyway, I want_to travel_around_and see something of the world before_I marry_and_(h)ave kids." She was_68_at the time!

Chapter 5: Over to you 3

1. /ʃiː kləʊzd n lɒkt ðə dɔːz/
   Assimilation: *-ed* and *–s* suffixes conditioned by preceding voiced or unvoiced sounds.

2. /juː dʒəs sɪt ðeə fə rə fjuː ˈmɪnɪts/
   Elision: final /t/ of *just*. Linking: /r/ between *for* and *a*.

3. /tel ɪm tə gəʊ wəˈweɪ/
   Linking: loss of aspiration on *him* and link with preceding /l/; linking /w/ after *go*.

4. /hiː jɪznt ʃʊə wɒt ɪʃ ʃeəz ə wɜːθ/
   Linking: /j/ between *he* and *isn't*. Regressive assimilation: /ʃ/ of *shares* modifies consonant of *his*. Weak form: *are* reduced to /ə/. An alternative transcription of *sure* is /ʃɔː/.

5. /juː mʌs bɪ mæd tʊ wiːvn θɪŋk əˈbaʊt ɪt/
   Elision: final /t/ of *must*. Linking: /w/ between *to* and *even*: *think_about_it* all linked. Second syllable of *even* could be transcribed with schwa instead of a syllabic consonant.

Chapter 6: Over to you 1

1. Falling tone. The speaker has given a straight answer and has nothing more to add.
2. Rise-fall for strong emotion. The speaker expresses (or possibly simulates) shock and indignation.
3. Rising tone. The second speaker invites the first to proceed.
4. Level, level then rise-fall. The third question causes offence.
5. Fall-rise. The second speaker agrees with reservation.

Chapter 6: Over to you 2

|| the ˌfirst of ˎ⁄april || which is the ˌday for ˈpractical ˎ⁄jokes || is our ˎwedding anniˌversary ||

Chapter 7: Over to you 1

1. /fep/ 2. /fiːp/ 3. /waɪb/ 4. /wɪb/ 5. /ˈmʌkʃn/ 6. /ˈmuːʃn/ 7. /ˈkleɪbɪəs/ 8. /ˈfæbɪəs/

If you have opted for these pronunciations it means that, consciously or unconsciously, you have applied some fairly reliable spelling rules.

Chapter 7: Over to you 2

The three-letter words all have a short vowel. With the addition of *e*, the short vowel is converted either into a diphthong (/eɪ/ in *hate*, /aɪ/ in *site*, /əʊ/ in *hope*) or into a long vowel (/iː/ in *Pete* or the approximant consonant /j/ + /uː/ in *tune*). Leaving aside the technical terminology, however, there is another way of stating the rule that is easier to remember and, from a practical point of view, more useful. The names of the alphabetical letters of the vowels *a*, *e*, *i*, *o* and *u* are pronounced /eɪ/, /iː/, /aɪ/, /əʊ/ and /juː/, precisely the sounds that we hear in *hate*, *Pete*, *site*, *hope* and *tune*. We can say, therefore, that adding *e* causes the vowel to be pronounced like its alphabetical name.

Chapter 7: Over to you 3

When they are followed by a single consonant + the *–ion* suffix, *a*, *e*, *o* and *u* are pronounced like the names of the alphabetical letters (although *u* is /uː/ rather than /juː/). When they are followed by two consonants – *st*, *ct* or *pt* – they are short vowels. The rule applies with other suffixes, such as *–ial* (*racial* vs *substantial*) or *–ious* (*bumptious* vs *dubious*).

This rule is a little less reliable. It doesn't work for the vowel *i* (*vision* and *mission* both have short /ɪ/). Neither does it work if the single consonant is *x* (*complexion* and *noxious* have short vowels).

Chapter 7: Over to you 4

/ˈdɪərəst ˈkriːtʃə ɪn krɪˈeɪʃn
ˈstʌdi ˈɪŋglɪʃ prəˌnʌnsɪˈeɪʃn
aɪ wɪl tiːtʃ juː ɪn maɪ vɜːs
saʊndz laɪk kɔːps kɔː hɔːs ænd wɜːs
aɪ wɪl kiːp juː ˈsuːzi ˈbɪzi
meɪk jɔː hed wɪð hiːt grəʊ ˈdɪzi
tɪə ɪn aɪ jɔː dres wɪl teə
səʊ ʃæl aɪ əʊ hɪə maɪ ˈpreə/

n.b. This transcription gives the full forms of all syllables. The phenomena of linking, assimilation and elision are ignored.

SUGGESTIONS FOR FURTHER READING

For those seeking a more detailed introduction to the issues covered in this book, an excellent text is Peter Roach's *English Phonetics and Phonology* (Cambridge University Press).

Specifically for phonetics, the next step might be *Phonetics*, also by Peter Roach (Oxford University Press).

Two important texts on connected speech and intonation are *Pronunciation for Advanced Learners of English* by David Brazil (Cambridge University Press) and *English Intonation* by J.C. Wells (Cambridge University Press).

Recommended texts on pronunciation are *Pronunciation* by Clement Laroy (Oxford University Press) and *Better English Pronunciation* by J.D. O'Connor (Cambridge University Press).

Two extremely useful texts for teachers of English are *Sound Foundations* by Adrian Underhill (Macmillan) and *How to Teach Pronunciation* by Gerald Kelly (Pearson Longman). Ann Baker has also written two practical guides for teachers: at elementary level *Tree or Three* and at intermediate level *Ship or Sheep* (both Cambridge University Press).

People interested in the pronunciation of American English could start with Judy B. Gilbert's *Clear Speech from the Start* and *Clear Speech* (Cambridge University Press).

An excellent dictionary of pronunciation is the *Cambridge English Pronouncing Dictionary*.

INDEX

Affricate 13
Allophone 8
Alveolar ridge 9
Approximant 15, 17
Articulator 8
Assimilation 33

Clear *l* 16
Cockney 12, 57, 58
Consonant cluster 22
Continuant 13

Dark *l* 16
Diphthong 22

Elision 36, 37
Estuary English 56-59

Fortis 11
Fricative 11

Glottal plosive or Glottal stop 57
Glottis 9

Hard palate 9
High-rise terminals 54-56

International Phonetic Alphabet (IPA) 8
Intonation 39-45

Juncture 35

Lenis 11
Lateral 15
Linking 34, 35

Nasal 9, 13

Phoneme	8
Phonemic Transcription	8
Phonetics	7
Phonology	7
Plosive	13
Prescriptivism	53
Received Pronunciation (RP)	4, 56
Rhythm	25, 30
Semivowel	15, 17
Soft palate	9
Stress	28-30
Syllabic consonant	27
Syllable	25, 26
Tone unit	41, 42
Tonic syllable	41, 42
Triphthong	22
Uptalk	54-56
Uvula	9
Velum	9, 13
Vocal cords	9
Voicing	10

www.ingramcontent.com/pod-product-compliance
Ingram Content Group UK Ltd.
Pitfield, Milton Keynes, MK11 3LW, UK
UKHW051249180426
11947UKWH00020B/1608